Amazon Dream

Roberta Allen

City Lights

San Francisco

Cover design by Rex Ray
Cover photograph by Roberta Allen
Book design by Amy Scholder

Typography by Harvest Graphics

Library of Congress Cataloging-in-Publication Data

Allen, Roberta.
      Amazon dream / by Roberta Allen.
          p.   cm.
      ISBN 0-87286-270-4
      1.   Allen, Roberta.   2.   Amazon River Valley —
   Description and travel.   3.   Peru — Description and travel.
   4.   Allen, Roberta — Journeys — Amazon River Valley.
   5.   Allen, Roberta.   I.   Title.
F3425.A45   1993
918.1'10463 — dc20   92-24972
                                                                         CIP

City Lights Books are available to bookstores through our primary
distributor: Subterranean Company. P. O. Box 160, 265 S. 5th St., Monroe,
OR 97456. 503-847-5274. Toll-free orders 800-274-7826. FAX 503-847-6018.
Our books are also available through library jobbers and regional distributors.
For personal orders and catalogs, please write to City Lights Books,
261 Columbus Avenue, San Francisco CA 94133.

CITY LIGHTS BOOKS are edited by Lawrence Ferlinghetti and
Nancy J. Peters and published at the City Lights Bookstore,
261 Columbus Avenue, San Francisco, CA 94133.

ACKNOWLEDGEMENTS

I wish to thank Peter Koepke for sharing his expertise about Shipibo art and the Shipibo people. I also wish to thank him for being an inspiration for this trip: through our conversations the journey took shape in my mind. For their helpful suggestions on my early manuscript, I wish to thank Joel Agee, David Gurewich, and Jaime Manrique. More helpful criticism on later versions came from John Ash, April Bernard, Frederick Ted Castle, and Maggie Paley.

In these pages, I have tried to preserve a little piece of the Peruvian Amazon, to preserve what this place was to me. The Peruvian Amazon as I saw it in the fall of 1987 no longer exists. Foreigners I knew have fled from the Sendero Luminoso and Tupac Amaru terrorists. Other people were not so lucky. The mayor of a village where I stayed was assassinated on the waterfront by a young boy on a motorbike. In the hotel in that village I had worried about cockroaches. If I had been there later, I would have heard the sound of machine-gun fire at night, and in the morning, I would have seen dead bodies on the road. The man who ran the camp where I spent the first part of my trip is said to be somewhere in Brazil. On the lake, the lodge where I slept has been dismantled. The jungle has changed, and will continue to change. I have tried to capture a moment of the flux.

Most of the names in this book have been changed.

PHOTOGRAPHS
BY ROBERTA ALLEN

1

By some miracle, amid the crowds scrambling through the airport in Lima, I recognize Dr. Jorge Gonzales, Peru's ex-Minister of Health. I remembered the shape of his bald head from the snapshot his daughter showed me. He says I just missed meeting his friend, the writer, Mario Vargas Llosa, who was waiting for his son who had arrived on my plane from New York. Two burly guards part the sea of people to let us pass. More guards hold open the doors leading to the street. I hadn't expected this red carpet treatment.

Dr. Gonzales drives me to his home in an expensive Lima suburb where his daughter, an acquaintance of mine, has arranged for me to stay with her family overnight. Tomorrow my plane flies to

Iquitos in the Peruvian Amazon.

In the Mercedes, Dr. Gonzales says in a confidential tone, as though someone else might hear, "I found out last night that our president, Alan García, suffers from manias!"

"Manias?" I say, not quite sure what he means.

"Yes, manias! He's been hospitalized several times. Our president is loco!" he says, with an ironic laugh. "But we have to keep him in office until the next elections to save democracy in Peru."

For the last two years, the youthful Alan García has been a very popular president. A leader who was left of center came as a welcome change after the conservative six-year rule of Fernando Belaude Terry and the twelve-year dictatorship of Juan Velasco before him. But despite his popularity, the country is plagued by a huge national debt, inflation is rising, and poverty is growing after a brief moment of prosperity.

Before I left New York, Dr. Gonzales' daughter told me that friends of her father had been killed by terrorists' bombs last week near her parents' house, so I am not surprised to see a soldier with a submachine gun posted in a guardhouse on the corner. The huge Doberman pinscher, however, barking on the roof of Dr. Gonzales' house, brings the threat of terrorism *too* close to home.

The Sendero Luminoso or Shining Path, the best known of several terrorist groups, founded by Abimael Guzman, a former philosophy professor in Ayacucho, recruits its members from the poorest parts of Peru. Committed to the self-rule of the peasantry, they are Maoists, shunned by other Communists worldwide. On election day in 1980, they launched a "people's war" by hanging dead dogs from lampposts in Lima to protest China's treatment of the Gang of Four. In 1985, they welcomed President García with bombings and assassinations. A reign of terror began when the Shining Path joined forces with the Tupac Amaru Revolutionary Movement (MRTA), a smaller urban-based group. Together they bombed embassies, department stores, hotels and theaters, kidnapped businessmen, and killed military and police officers, civilians, and politicians. When imprisoned terrorists staged an uprising, it was suppressed by the military, which executed prisoners who surrendered. Both the leftist terrorists and the military who murder suspected collaborators in peasant villages are working to destroy democracy.

In Dr. Gonzales' library of rare books, however, Peru's terrorists seem light-years away. Seated in an overstuffed chair, sipping Scotch, he tells me about a trip he made to the Amazon when he was a young man. Most upper class Peruvians wouldn't set foot in the Amazon. To them, the jungle is the armpit of the earth. He rattles off the names of diseases he encountered as though he had been there yesterday. Every disease he mentions other than cholera is still a menace: yellow fever, malaria, typhoid, tuberculosis, hepatitis, amoebic dysentery, worms. There are other diseases that he hasn't mentioned: leprosy; Chagas' disease, which may cause cardiac and digestive dysfunction twenty years after a beetle bite; onchocerciasis, which causes blindess; and leishmaniasis, which causes the disintegration of the nose and palate, to name a few. There are also biting flies, ticks, chiggers, bees, wasps, stinging ants, and botflies whose larvae, imbedded in human hosts, may mature into inch-long maggots.

I assure Dr. Gonzales I have all the innoculations I need, and, in addition, I carry a portable pharmacy in my duffel with everything from insect repellent to antibiotics, shampoo for lice, and a snake-bite kit that my friend Kenneth in New York insisted that I bring, though when I read the instructions at home, I could hardly imagine sucking venom from my arm. I even carry a malaria pill for a new strain resistant to quinine, which should only be taken if you are sure you have the disease; otherwise, the pill can be fatal.

"Why are you making this trip?" Dr. Gonzales asks.

"I fell in love with the jungle six months ago on a trip through Peru with a guide and two other Americans," I tell him. "We weren't in the Amazon long, but when I came home, I couldn't stop thinking about the jungle. In New York, I met this man named Kenneth, an expert on Shipibo Indian art. He's been making trips to their villages for years, buying pottery and textiles. Listening to his stories made me want to go back and see more. I had seen one Shipibo village; as an artist, I felt instantly attracted to their art."

In that Shipibo village, I saw giggling women and children sitting on bark floors in unwalled thatch huts, surrounded by dust and mud and forest. I gazed into faces that were more than foreign. Who are these people? I wondered. I held in my hands a painted bowl. The delicate lines, the muted colors, the geometric patterns related to my own work. How could I, a New York artist, and a tribe of Amazonian Indians share the same aesthetics? I saw their art through the eyes of my culture. How they perceived their art was a mystery to me; nevertheless, I felt their work was a link between us.

"So you are going to the Amazon to buy Shipibo art?" Dr. Gonzales says.

"Well, not exactly. I'd like to find some pottery to take home, but that's not my main reason." I hesitate.

I find it hard to tell a stranger that I have dreamt of the Amazon all of my life, that the Amazon has always meant freedom to me, to live without rules, to do as I please.

I was an only child in Manhattan, raised in an overprotective home, mainly by my mother and grandmother, who never let me out of their sight. I first learned about jungles in the Museum of Natural History, where my grandmother often took me after school. I longed to escape from my mother's house. I longed to be free. I watched *Ramar of the Jungle* faithfully on TV and envied his adventures. My only adventures were on Sundays when my father took me to the park. In my fantasies, I was Rima, the jungle girl in *Green Mansions,* the novel by W.H. Hudson. Like Rima, I was a free spirit, at one with all the creatures of the forest. I could climb trees and get dirty. I could play with animals and sleep in a tree house I built myself. When we lived in the suburbs briefly, I played alone in vacant lots, which were my jungles. I named them *South America, Africa, Asia.* Surrounded by overgrown weeds, broken furniture, motor parts, and mysterious odds and ends, I explored a secret world where invisible natives kept me company.

Before my first trip through Peru six months ago, I never thought seriously about going to the Amazon. My traveling had been limited for some years to exhibitions abroad, then short trips alone to Latin America. I used to see myself as a gypsy. In fact, years ago, I lived like a gypsy with my husband; for several years we roamed through Europe and part of North Africa. When we divorced, I roamed through Mexico alone.

Six months ago, I was feeling constrained in New York. It was time for a change of scene.

I allowed my friends, who were appalled by the idea of my going alone to Peru, to talk me into taking a tour with a guide. Peru is dangerous! they said. There are terrorists! It didn't take much to convince me.

On that trip the Amazon was our last stop. There, my old dream came alive. Sheltered by walls of vegetation thick with life, I felt as though I was a guest in nature's grandest house, even though the canals were muddy and the muted browns and greens of the dry season looked nothing like the jungle scenes I remembered from movies. Nevertheless, the trees seemed so familiar. I felt as though I had always known these trees, that all my life I had been waiting to see them. I was discovering in the world a dream that was real.

In answer to Dr. Gonzales' question, I reply, "I just want to be there again before the jungle is destroyed."

In the jungle near Pucallpa, a rapidly growing city, tracts of forest are already destroyed, life in Indian villages is changing, and I am afraid that fragile world will be gone if I wait too long to return.

"So this is a vacation," Dr. Gonzales says. "The Amazon is not the sort of place I would go on vacation," he laughs.

"I guess you could call it a vacation," I say to him.

"Do you have a hotel reservation in Iquitos?" he asks.

"No, I'll find a hotel when I get there."

"So you have no fixed schedule?" he asks, eyes wide with amazement.

"Well, I heard about a conservation camp in the jungle, run by a man in Iquitos. I want to go there, and I want to return to Yarinacocha, the lake near the Shipibo villages. I'm bringing letters to some of Kenneth's friends who live by the lake."

"What a gringa our daughter has sent us!" Dr. Gonzales laughs. "I've never met an American before who travels without a fixed schedule." In a serious tone, he adds, "You must call me if you have any problem. Let me know when you will return."

I'm sure Dr. Gonzales is glad I'm not his daughter.

2

How amazing to land in the Amazon after only an hour or so on a plane! A trip from Lima to Iquitos used to take three months. Before a road through the Andes connected Lima with Pucallpa, a town 600 miles south of Iquitos, one had to travel around northern South America, across Panama, and down the Atlantic to the Amazon River to reach Iquitos. The only other route was over the Andes with Indians and mules.

Surrounded by water and jungle, Iquitos, Peru's largest Amazon city, with more than a quarter of a million people, is still remote. The port, 2300 miles from the Atlantic, is further inland than any other port in the world. Besides the Amazon River, which is also called the Marañón here, there are two Amazon tributaries: the

Nanay and the Itaya. But only one paved road extends out of town and ends in jungle about twenty miles away.

As the taxi drives toward the center from the airport, I feel light-headed, intoxicated. The hot, sweet-smelling air in the darkness gives me the sensation of riding through a greenhouse with my eyes closed. A piece of rope holds the cab door in place. Moths spin round yellow lights on the road. The lights multiply on the outskirts of town. Dogs and barefoot children dart in and out of shadows. Hazy figures linger in doorways and move in slow motion behind swirling clouds of yellow dust. The children's laughter seems muffled. In the soft yellow glow, the town is ephemeral, dreamlike, faint as an old film.

The hotel that I chose from my guidebook is situated at the end of a side street on a high bank beside the Amazon River.

The manager, a squat woman with suspicious eyes, leads me through the entrance and out along a narrow path through a garden with enormous red flowers between two rows of bungalows. The air is filled with the monotonous medley of cicadas.

The room is not quite what I expected, but for the price I'm paying, I guess I shouldn't have expected more. The walls seem as thin as cardboard, and cold water trickles from the shower, but the fan works, and the windows are screened. I wonder why a huge plastic bucket, filled with water is standing by the sink: scores of minute insects float on the surface. I hope I won't have to wash in that water. A thin stream flows from the tap when I try it.

When I think of the white satin sheets I slept on last night, Dr. Gonzales' house seems like a dream. This bed is pulled away from the wall so creatures won't crawl on me while I sleep. The room looks clean, but I examine the floors, the walls, the ceiling. Am I looking for snakes? Spiders? Scorpions?

It's too early to sleep so I head toward Iquitos' main square, the Plaza de Armas, a few blocks from my hotel. Along the way, the houses are shuttered and silent, so I am surprised to see an art school in session. Inside the doorway, small dark students smile at me shyly as they sketch still lifes on easels. I walk along a damp, moldy corridor with tufts of green growing through cracks in the floor. This school is an Amazon version of a traditional European art academy.

A heavy-set man with several gold teeth approaches me, and introduces himself as Guillermo, a teacher here.

"This is the only art school in the Peruvian Amazon," he says in Spanish, proudly, offering me a stool under the bare bulb in the dim corridor.

Half a dozen men in baggy trousers, who seem to materialize from nowhere, gather round us. They have few teeth, but specks of gold glitter in their mouths when they smile. I am frightened for a moment.

Who are these men? They look too old to be students, but Guillermo says they are in their final year.

"I'm an artist, too," I tell them, "and a writer."

"What kind of art do you make?" Guillermo asks.

"I draw and paint," I tell him.

"Two years ago," he says, "we had a blond woman, an Austrian artist, teaching here."

What happened to her?" I ask.

"She left," he says. "She got fed up. Materials are so difficult to get from Lima, and so expensive! We always run out of canvas and paint."

From his pocket he pulls out crumpled newspaper clippings and proudly shows me yellowing pictures of large murals on public walls, murals with social themes, painted by his students in the style of the great Mexican muralists.

Guillermo invites me to view the paintings in a nearby studio. Inspired by Dali and Magritte, surreal canvases hang askew on the rotting walls. I see no jungle scenes, but the jungle permeates the air. Perhaps the Amazon offers exciting subject matter only to those who don't live here. I can understand the appeal of surrealism in this dreamlike town.

Founded as a Jesuit mission in the early seventeenth century, Iquitos offically became a town in 1863, but that didn't stop Indians in the surrounding jungle from raiding the city.

With the help of warships from Lima, Iquitos survived the early Indian attacks, but didn't distinguish itself until the end of the nineteenth century, when the city became a great rubber town. At the height of the rubber boom, fifteen thousand people lived here. A host of foreigners, especially Europeans, came to buy rubber and to sell goods and services. All the luxuries of the Victorian era filled the mansions that sprang up along the Malecón, the grand promenade by the river.

My first glimpse of Iquitos in early morning after a storm doesn't disappoint me. The contradictions I expect to find in a town carved out of jungle are everywhere evident.

On streets glistening with puddles, I step over large black beetles lying on their backs, their legs stabbing the air. Pekinese dogs nervously bark and seem to chase invisible enemies. Rickshaws powered by motorcycles speed down streets, barely avoiding collisions. These frenzied rickshaws are a stark contrast to the otherwise lethargic pace of the city. Small mud and brick buildings in dirty peeling pastel shades line the streets. Goods from small shops spill over onto the sidewalks.

A few reminders of Iquitos' heyday remain. Off the Plaza de Armas stands the iron house designed by Eiffel and transported in pieces from Paris by a rubber baron. The yellow cathedral in the square has a fairy-tale quality. Adorning discolored walls of decaying colonial mansions, brightly patterned tiles from Italy and Portugal gleam like precious jewels.

During the rubber boom, hordes of drifters who dreamed of owning mansions ended up as little more than slaves. Indebted to rubber barons, they tapped rubber under miserable conditions. As American and European markets demanded more rubber and workers became scarce, export companies employed native laborers. The greed and cruelty of the rubber barons caused the deaths of many Indians.

The worst attrocities were committed along the Putumayo River, an Amazon tributary, by a rubber baron named Julio Cesar Arana who operated out of Iquitos. Using armed force, Arana gained control of Indian rubber gatherers along the disputed border region between Peru and Colombia, and was ready for large-scale expansion with British capital by 1907.

An eyewitness account written for a London magazine by an American engineer, briefly imprisoned by Arana's men, prompted the British government to send Roger Casement, then consulate general in Rio de Janeiro, to investigate.

The British were unaware they were financing the genocide of Indians, who were subject to extreme torture. In 1912, Casement reported that at least half of the 30,000 Indians in the Putumayo region had been killed between 1901 and 1911. The Indians controlled by Arana were whipped, starved, burned alive and fed to dogs, not just to punish them when latex quotas weren't met, but also for amusement.

Ironically, Casement was later executed as a German spy, though homosexuality seems to have been his major crime. Arana, credited with Iquitos' economic rise, remains a hero: the charges against him dismissed as lies.

After 1912, when it was discovered that transplanted rubber trees could be grown more economically on Southeast Asian plantations, prices for rubber fell, and by the 1920's, Iquitos had returned to jungle lethargy.

The town discovered barbasco in the 1930s, a root long used as fish poison by the Indians. As an insecticide, barbasco was sold profitably on the world market. The United States still imports barbasco as well as timber, oil, and other products.

In the late seventies, oil exploration and the building of a pipeline to the Pacific spurred the economy, but this period of prosperity was short-lived. Drug smuggling, however, is still going strong.

Until the rubber boom collapse, Iquitos was tied to Western Europe. Now the Iquiteños dream of Miami rather than Liverpool, where the British Booth Line once sailed with luxuries bound for Iquitos.

As I head toward the office of Pepe Morales, a man who runs a conservation project and arranges jungle trips, I pass the eyesore of Iquitos, a charred, ten-story hulk capped with radio towers, looming behind the Plaza de Armas. Trees grow out of the eighth-story windows. I look through my guidebook for a description of this monstrosity but find none, although it seems to be Iquitos' tallest building besides the cathedral. The first two floors of the otherwise abandoned structure are occupied by social security offices.

On Putumayo Street, off the Plaza de Armas, signs for jungle tours compete for attention. I was warned about these tours offering caged animals, discotheques, and visits to villages where mestizos dress up like Indians, sell native weapons as souvenirs, and demonstrate their marksmanship with blowguns.

I had heard that Pepe Morales was the only one who ran serious jungle trips from Iquitos. He had been recommended by several people in the States, including a biologist who worked here for several years, but no one I spoke to had ever met him.

At his office, a barefoot boy tells me he is at home, asleep.

Pepe arrives thirty minutes later, however, after being informed that an American writer was here to see him. Before I left New

York, I proposed a story about Pepe's camp to a magazine editor who sounded interested, although I couldn't give her many details.

Pepe is not what I expected. I sense something devious about him which makes me apprehensive. I wonder if those people in the States who recommended him would have second thoughts if they saw him now.

A mestizo in his late twenties, he is short and thickset, with a hawklike nose and heavy lips. When he shakes my hand, he exudes an oily charm he probably reserves for tourists.

"Come," he says in his oily voice. "We will have a drink next door."

I feel like the fly lured by the spider as he leads me inside a dim cafe. But I tell myself I could be wrong. I try to reserve judgment despite what I feel. Also, I am curious. I've never had a drink with anyone like him before. He is someone I'd have dealings with only in a place like this. He is interesting to me like a rare species of bird.

As I tell him about the story I'd like to write for the magazine, his nose wrinkles and his mouth curls in a smile.

"Just when I gave up hope to save my project, *you* come. You make my dream come true!" he says in a voice that makes me think of swamps and worms and other squirmy things. "I am so depressed I sleep round the clock. I must get money for the project. The project is my life!" he says, placing his hand over his heart.

"I doubt my story will save your project," I say, trying to sound realistic. "I don't even know if the magazine will publish it."

"But you give me hope," he says in his oiliest voice.

I bet he performs like this for all the tourists. It's not personal, I decide, and breathe a little easier.

"I heard that you buy tame animals in Iquitos and return them to the jungle," I say.

He slides a pudgy hand through his thick black hair. "That is only part of my project," he says, in a voice that sounds more natural. "I retrain the animals with the help of two American volunteers who live at my camp. I taught them myself. They dedicate their lives to my project. But I get no help from the Peruvian government. I want to buy the preserve I rent from them. I have a six-year lease. If they are happy with my work, there is no problem. But I must get money! My jungle trips don't pay my costs. I have no money to build houses for the animals, so I have very few animals now. I cannot pay scientists to come. I need scientists to count and classify the birds, the animals, the fish, the plants, the trees."

He sounds serious.

From a briefcase he pulls out packs of Kodak prints taken at the preserve, which covers over 200,000 acres, he says. For a second, I glimpse a darkness in his face.

Before my eyes, he has transformed himself into a salesman. He is giving me a hard sell.

I sense he is capable of violence, but my New York instincts tell me I'm not in danger. To him, I'm just another tourist. His interest is only in selling me a jungle trip.

Despite the dim light and poor prints, I am impressed by pictures of horned screamers with spikes growing out of their foreheads, hawks, pink dolphins, monkeys, giant otters, caimans, fish, and enormous lily pads he says are six feet wide. He points out three strange looking fish which he claims have never been classified. "Habitat destruction", he tells me, "kills many species and causes others to retreat."

While showing me photos of smiling families in rags standing before thatched huts, he says proudly, "I built the first school in the region." He points out a wooden shack with a corrugated metal roof. "Now I want to build a clinic and an orphanage. I know what the villages need. I was born in the jungle. I was raised there."

"It looks very exciting," I say when he's finished his sales pitch. How dangerous can it be, I ask myself, with two Americans living there?

He is a very smooth talker. Before I know it, I am paying him in full. He's already persuaded me to stay twice as long as I'd planned.

"I will take you personally through the jungle and show you everything," he says, smiling. I wish he hadn't offered me this special bonus. I know he has guides who lead these trips.

"That's really not necessary," I say to him, but he has made up his mind.

"We leave tomorrow morning at nine. I will meet you at your hotel at 8:30," he says.

This trip may be more of an adventure than I bargained for.

3

I keep telling myself that Pepe was recommended, but I can't help feeling I've made a terrible mistake as I head toward the port and floating slum of Belén, with its thatched roofs rising about two miles from the center of town. To recreate nineteenth-century Belén for the film *Fitzcarraldo*, Herzog had only to eliminate the outboard motors.

The sight of the Mercado Belén, a vast claustrophobic maze of covered wooden stalls, drives Pepe from my thoughts. I see swarms of flies and mosquitoes. Blackened banana peels and oozing fruit float in the liquified mud of open sewers as I make my way through the crowds.

The Mercado Belén is the most important market in the

Peruvian lowland jungle, an enormous area where less than four people live on each square mile. Everything grown and gathered in forests, rivers, and fields is bought and sold here. The market is indispensable to those in small towns and settlements linked only by rivers. Here, produce is traded for soap, herbal medicine, sugar, kerosene, cloth, and notebooks. In Iquitos, with almost half of Peru's lowland people, almost six thousand vendors sell food and herbal medicine. Depending on supply, prices fluctuate wildly from day to day.

Fish, fowl, meat and fruit reek in the steaming air. Besides grapefruit called *toronjas,* and bananas, a staple brought here by the Spanish, many of the fruits look unfamiliar: some have prickly skins, others feel as tough as leather, still others are sold mashed in small plastic bags.

A fermented manioc paste called *masato,* used to make an alcoholic drink, is packed in green leaves on the ground.

I see many kinds of catfish, some with fantastic armor, others with thornlike scales or leopard spots. Some are large enough to require several men to carry them. The largest freshwater fish in the world, the giant *paiche,* comes from a family that can be traced back over a hundred million years. Some are eight feet long. Locals eat the freshwater fish in salted fillets dried in the sun.

The *paiche* isn't the only endangered creature in the market. The meat of river turtles is sold openly, too. Dried monkey meat is also for sale. There are laws to protect animals, but there are no police to enforce them; the Amazon is too large, so animals continue to be captured or killed for cash.

Beyond the dark cavern of canvas-covered booths, I glimpse shacks of weathered and roughly-sawn boards. Emerging into the light, the clutter of hovels with rotting roofs of dried gray thatch are sharply defined against the sky.

Windows and open doorways frame bare-chested men with

copper-colored skin lying in hammocks. Their children crawl around on all fours. Old sewing machines seem incongruous possessions in bare huts where women work in darkness, scraps of cloth on the floor.

I stop on the high bank by a steep flight of crumbling steps that descend to a vast sea of black slime; dung-like hills waver in the heat. A huge collapsed bridge of rotting planks and half-sunk logs stretches across this landscape of filth. Several seconds lapse before I recognize the large black birds as vultures. Pigs and chickens join the vultures feeding in the putrid mud while more vultures overhead eye the feast below. Barefoot boys chase each other through the muck. A small dark girl with a baby at her breast slowly crosses the bridge. On the other side, blackened huts on rafts and stilts stretch for miles.

I can't believe what I am seeing. I descend the first short flight of steps expecting to wake up from a dream. Nothing in the real world looks like this. This is what Hell must look like.

I feel ashamed of my intrusion, but no one else seems to care. Locals stroll slowly past me. Women nurse babies in doorways, and idle men drink Pepsi or Inca Cola in the shade.

Some of these people are detribalized Indians or descendents of the Indians who once lived along the major Amazon tributaries: there may have been more than six million in 1500, though only 200,000 survive today. Others are descendents of immigrants who came here during the rubber boom: these are mestizos of Indian and European blood, and outsiders from other parts of Peru or other Andean countries.

After the rubber boom, those who survived the hardships of rubber tapping found themselves penniless and adrift. Settlements were abandoned, people scattered, and new villages formed. Some adapted to the vagaries of export markets for other forest products, but minor booms for animal skins or rosewood oil ended quickly, disrupting their lives. Some remained along the rivers to farm while others wandered to Belén, looking for jobs.

But there are few jobs to be found here. The lucky ones find work as cargo carriers, and some women become maids or washer-women. Many drift back and forth from the villages to the city. The young, eager to come to Belén, may attend school for several years. The lack of schools and clinics in the villages often drives them to the city, but the deprivations they suffer here may be as bad as those they hoped to escape.

A barefoot girl with a baby in her arms murmurs something in my ear as she passes. When I turn, a man wearing glasses patched with tape beckons to me from his porch.

"Three boys are following you," he says, in Spanish, pointing to the top of the stairs. "They want to rob you."

I look up and see three boys grinning at me. Clutching my bag, I ask him, "Will you walk me out of the market to the main street?"

He shakes his head, no, even though I offer him money.

"Julio!" he shouts. A boy about fifteen emerges from the hut. "Take this gringa to the main street," he says.

Julio wants to know where I am from. "Are there big markets in New York?" he asks in Spanish.

"Yes," I reply.

"But everyone is rich?" he says.

"Not everyone. There are poor people who have no homes and sleep on the streets."

He looks at me and smiles slyly; he thinks I am putting him on.

Approaching the labyrinth of stalls, I change my mind. I don't want to give up. I came here to see the harbor.

"Is there a place where I can rent a boat to see the port?" I ask him.

"Yes," he says, and gestures for me to follow him.

I look behind me. I'm glad I don't see those three grinning boys.

Julio shows me high-water marks on the thatched roof shacks. The river rises thirty to thirty-five feet or more in the rainy season, which begins at the end of October and lasts until early April. The heaviest rains fall from December to March. During that time, it rains everyday, and sometimes continues for several days without stopping.

When the rains begin, those who can't afford to build new houses carry theirs to higher ground. Others float their houses on rafts. The houses on stilts look so flimsy, I wonder how many will stand after the rains.

As swarms of vultures circle overhead, I follow Julio over mounds of rotting banana peels until we reach the river where I try to keep my balance on the haphazard logs, the only walkways over the mud.

The Amazon, filled with sewage and sediment from the Andean highlands, looks like brown soup. Nevertheless, the river is used for bathing, drinking, swimming, washing clothes, watering animals, and as a latrine.

Several large, two-tiered river boats remind me of Mark Twain on the Mississippi. They listlessly sway in the water as slow-moving men in filthy trousers, weighed down by huge sacks, climb the garbage-strewn bank to the market.

Between clusters of houseboats, river buses and cargo boats, slender dugout canoes serve as water taxis. Julio talks to a boatboy, a handsome, healthy-looking child of ten or twelve.

"He will take you through the port for a dollar," Julio says to me.

I feel guilty hiring this child, but on the other hand I don't want to hire any of the men standing by their dugouts, looking at me, amused.

I open my wallet and pull out some bills to give Julio, but he shakes his head, no. I thank him profusely, and wonder what else I can offer when he walks away in the mud.

The river is a scene of frenetic activity. Pigs, chickens, and dogs run about the houseboats of families with as many as eight or nine children. Diving off rafts, screaming boys splash in the soupy water. Only the children are curious about me. Dr. Gonzales had said the child mortality rate is high in Peru, but the children look surprisingly healthy. "If they reach twelve, they survive," he told me. I wonder how they survive.

Women are busy washing clothes, or their offspring, while crowded river buses arrive from jungle settlements. Passengers carry wild fruit and live chickens to sell in the market.

Families with bundles pass in canoes as small as ours, with children bailing water to keep afloat.

Drums of petrol in floating gas stations balance precariously on rafts.

Over the years, businessmen have grown rich from their labor in the forests, but the lives of the river people have barely changed. I don't know how to reconcile the sickness, malnutrition, alcoholism, illiteracy, and unemployment that I know exists with the tremendous vitality I see around me. On this river, I feel an overwhelming sense of life.

4

When Pepe comes to my hotel this morning, I am in no condition to travel. I've been up all night with the runs. "No problem," Pepe says. "I come back tomorrow to see how you are." How relaxed he seems now that he has my money.

I feel comfortable lying in my little room which is beginning to feel like home. I'm glad I have this day to think things over. Sometimes getting sick is the only way I slow down. I'm not ready for Pepe and the jungle.

I try to make sense of what I've seen, but nothing fits, nothing makes sense. During the day, something sinister hangs in the air, something indefinable but heavy. I can't reconcile the menace I feel with the open, childlike smiles of strangers. I can't reconcile the sweet-smelling night with the decay that taints the city by day.

In daylight, I feel like a sleepwalker in someone else's dream. At night, I breathe easier. Night erases the harsh shadows, veils the wounds, hides the rot. At night I am close to my dream.

The hotel manager offers me pills when I tell her I am ill, which I decline. From experience I know that bottled water and rice is all I need.

I order rice in a little restaurant. Clearly, the young waitress has never served a gringa before. She can hardly keep from laughing when she takes my order. Staring at me while I eat, her shoulders shake, her hand covers her mouth.

In the hotel patio, the houseboys have a hummingbird in a wire mesh cage with the door open. They tell me the bird can't fly. One of them says there are hummingbirds only two centimeters long.

When I pass by again, the cage door is closed and the bird flies desperately from side to side in its prison. Its wings flutter like helicopter propellers in the air.

A storm is brewing. The patio lights are turned on early. The slate-colored sky looks as hard as stone. Thunder rumbles in the distance. The swish of leaves sounds like rising and falling tides. As though a door has opened, dark and light tones break loose in the sky, and I feel filled with joy and gratitude. A hummingbird, not much larger than a bumble bee, hovers in the air. The storm has passed, but the sight of a large black bat sends me scurrying to my room.

I can't sustain my joy. I'm restless. My little room begins to feel oppressive, but I'm too weak to go out again. I hear children's laughter through the thin walls. I see the sound breaking through a core of roots buried in mud. Everything feels dark and strange suddenly. Why did I come here? I remember my excitement when Kenneth showed me a photo of Belén: here was life in the raw.

Perhaps this life is too raw.

Like a miracle my fears and doubts have vanished by morning. I am at Pepe's office, ready to leave, but he says the boat won't be ready until tomorrow.

"What do you mean it's not ready?" I ask. "It was ready yesterday, wasn't it?" Patience is not my strong suit.

"The boys are working on it," Pepe says, in a flat voice. "You should rest another day. If you are sick in the jungle, there is no doctor, no medicine."

Being serenaded by my taxi driver on the dusty road to Quistacocha doesn't ameliorate my disappointment. Quistacocha, the site of a zoo and a museum, is sixteen kilometers out of town on a lake. My taxi looks like a car abandoned after a crash on a New York street.

This zoo is like no other I've seen. More than half the dirty, wire mesh cages are empty. Walking on ramps of rotting planks, I peer into pools of slimy water for signs of life, but many of the pools are empty, too.

I am fascinated, however, by three tiny, sharp-clawed, hissing marmosets with piercing eyes. One is small enough to fit in the palm of my hand, but they are not what I would call cute. Without prehensile tails, they can't swing from branches. They move like squirrels. They seem so alien, but so alive. I'm amazed that we breathe the same air.

On a small island, I watch a howler monkey parade back and forth like a little king. The sound of one howler — the largest monkey in the Americas — may be heard for more than a mile. When they roam in bands, foraging for fruit in the jungle at night, their roars are said to be deafening. I'm glad this one is silent.

Capybaras, the world's largest rodents, look like guinea pigs the size of sheep. Several of them stand beside a scummy pool while another moves swiftly through the water. Their partially webbed toes enable them to swim almost as well as fish.

The snake cages are empty except for an anaconda, the most feared snake in the region beside the fer-de-lance. This one is coiled and asleep. Under the jungle lodge where I stayed six months ago, the owners kept a caged anaconda which was fed one live chicken a week. Anacondas suffocate their prey. We weren't there on its feeding day so we missed that spectacle. There's no food in this cage or any of the cages I've seen. Too late I remember the biologist in New York who lived in Iquitos. She told me to bring food to this zoo because the animals are barely fed.

On my way out, I almost miss the museum, a small shack near the entrance, displaying animal embryos in formaldehyde jars. I am reminded of a fair years ago in Amsterdam where embryos of two-headed calves were displayed in jars like these under a circus tent. I have always had a taste for the bizarre.

Fairs, circuses, and amusement parks I visited with my father when I was a child often come to mind here. I feel the same excitement now that I felt then. There are moments when I think Iquitos is a giant sideshow.

The museum in town is no less macabre than the museum in Quistacocha. In a damp dungeon-like room with bare bulbs, stuffed animals wear their fiercest expressions under layers of dust. The museum looks like an abandoned prop room for a horror movie set.

At the end of the day, the Amazon river turns a copper color, with patches of silver-blue. Golden light fires the hotel patio, the plants, the trees. I walk out along the Malecón, the promenade by the water.

An elderly man with thick spectacles standing beside me introduces himself as the Technical Director of Drinking Water. Seeing my scepticism, he shows me his card. The only drinkable water in Iquitos, however, comes in bottles I buy at the store. Drinking tap water is the surest way to get amoebic dysentery. I think of the dark slimy water in Belén, two miles away. I am still haunted by the image of that bridge.

"Do you know Belén well?" I ask him.

"No, no, nooo!" he says, wagging his finger and shaking his head. "You mustn't go there! Belén is bad! Very bad! Many drugs!

"My son lives in Pucallpa. That's a better place than this. There they work. Here they sleep. Pucallpa is the town of the future. Mark my words!"

Idle men lean on the balustrade; behind them a crumbling slope leads to Amazon mud. Women, some in tight pants, giggle as the men make remarks. Some call out to me. I begin to wonder if I'm the only tourist in town as I watch a patch of violet sky darken. Streaks of iridescent rose fade. I wish I could share this view with someone, but despite moments like this, I prefer traveling alone. I am more aware of my surroundings, more in touch with my sensations. When I traveled through Guatemala with a fellow artist, I remember walking through the jungle complaining about the New York art world!

Later, Pepe calls to tell me we can't leave tomorrow after all. The boat hasn't returned.

"Returned?" I say. "Returned from where? I thought it was being fixed this morning."

"It broke down somewhere on the river," he says, ignoring the irritation in my voice. "We leave the day after tomorrow."

I begin to wonder if we will leave at all.

While writing in my journal, I hear someone behind me on the hotel patio call out, "Hello."

I turn around and see a tall man in dusty clothes, his face and arms bronzed by the sun, his dark hair streaked with gold. I wonder if I am dreaming.

"I don't want to bother you," he says with a heavy European accent.

"You're not bothering me," I reply. "Did you just arrive?"

"Yes. I've just been through a nightmare," he says. "I've been traveling through South America for a year. I am a filmmaker from Münich. I am on my way back to Manaus to catch a plane to Germany. Now, at the end of my trip, my baggage is lost! I can't believe it!"

"Where was it lost?" I ask.

"In Lima. My bags were put on the wrong plane. I just spent hours at the airport here while officials tried to find them. They think my bags may be on a plane to Panama. I won't know until tomorrow morning. If they're not, I'll have to fly back to Lima, and lose my charter flight to Germany. But I won't go home until I've made every effort to find them."

"That is a nightmare!"

"I can't bear to think about it, but I can't think of anything else. All the little things you collect while you travel — they are irreplaceable! Fortunately, I sent my journals home every two months, and my current journal I have with me," he says, holding up the book in his hand. "Is there some place to have a drink nearby?

"On the Malecón, by the river," I reply.

"Will you join me?" he asks.

I close my journal.

Walking toward the Malecón with Gerhart, I realize I have my wish. I can share the view of the Amazon River, after all. Unfortunately, the river and the sky seem locked behind a black wall. Only a few scattered stars break through and glimmer intermittently.

"I love the smell of the air at night," I say to him, as we sit in a cafe.

"So do I," he replies. "Even if I was blind I would recognize the jungle by this special smell. So sickly sweet. I remembered it from Manaus the moment I arrived."

"A year is a long time to travel in South America. Did you travel alone all that time?" I ask.

"I met many people. Sometimes I joined up with one or two, but only for a brief time. There were weeks when I saw no one but peasants in little mountain villages. But I had my journal to keep me company."

"What will you do with your journals?" I ask.

"I don't know yet. I am so tired now. So many images pass through my mind. I've seen so much. It's time I went home."

"My trip is just beginning," I muse.

"Yes, it's wonderful when everything is ahead of you, and scary, too." Gerhart closes his eyes for a moment. "I still must deal with this nightmare tomorrow. I must leave for the airport very early. Aside from meeting you, this has been the worst day of my trip."

Walking back to the hotel, I'm sorry our paths crossed now. How nice it would have been to spend some time with him.

"I wish you a wonderful journey," he says at my door.

5

On board Pepe's motorboat, which looks more like a ship-
wreck, I sit between oil drums, the wind in my face,
happy at last to be leaving after a delay of three more
days. Paula, a young American volunteer who lives at Pepe's camp,
told me this morning at the office that Pepe was too busy to guide
me, but he sent his apologies. "That's too bad," I replied, and
thanked my lucky stars!

Paula, who would stand out as a beauty even on a California
beach, joins me on the eighty-mile trip west to the Yarapa River.
"What brought you here?" I ask her.

"I made a trip to Pepe's camp last year," she says. "I worked in a
zoo in the States, but working with animals in the jungle is some-

thing else. I had to come back," she says, grinning.

"Do you have any problem with the men here?" I ask. "You're the only blond I've seen."

"No one really bothers me when I travel alone. I've traveled for fifteen hours in a hammock on the deck of a *collectivo* that stops at every settlement between Iquitos and the village near the camp, and never had any problem," she says. "When I first came to the camp, the cook tried to crawl inside my mosquito net at night, but after a month he gave up."

As Paula dozes in the sun, I suddenly recall seeing her a couple of days ago, laughing in the plaza with a group of men. She was wearing shorts. I thought she was too brave.

Once we pass the town and Padre Isla, the island dividing the Amazon, a smattering of small farms line the bank. As we speed upriver, few birds disturb the solitude.

The Amazon River, with its 1,100 tributaries (ten of them larger than the Rhine) and its network of lakes, lagoons, and streams, is like a great web of waters that unite in an eastward flow to the Atlantic and nourish an area two-thirds the size of the United States. The Amazon region, bordered by Guiana in the north, the Andes in the west, Brazil in the south, and the Atlantic in the east, includes parts of nine nations. The forests drained by the river, have been relatively undisturbed for more than a hundred million years. Not even glaciers from the Ice Age touched them.

The Amazon is the largest river in the world in volume. Arising high in the Peruvian Andes, the river flows 4000 miles to the sea, discharging twenty percent of the world's freshwater. Only the Nile is longer, but not by much. During the rainy season, parts of the river may swell to thirty-five miles in width. The mouth of the Amazon is two hundred miles wide.

Francisco Orellana, the first white explorer to travel down the Amazon from Ecuador to the Atlantic in 1542, named the river partly from Greek myth. According to his chronicler, Carvajal, Orellana and his men battled fierce warrior women. Carvajal claimed these women were brave captains and skillful archers. In tales Orellana and his chronicler heard upriver, these tall blond warriors lived apart from men in cities of gold and bore children with men they kidnapped from nearby villages. Male offspring were killed.

The straggly green growth along the banks doesn't look like a landscape where myths are made. The river looks deceptively narrow in places because of the islands, some miles long, that obscure the banks. Young trees grow like stubble on the scalps of these islands.

Long stretches of empty sandbanks glaring white against a brilliant sky loom on the horizon, while smaller islands of vegetation drift by us.

On a near bank, rice fields sway like millions of graceful green feathers edging the shore. Rice is grown when the river is low, and harvested before the rains. Unpredictable floods can wipe out the crop.

The river is always changing. The contours are unrecognizable from one year to the next: each rainy season the river cuts off giant chunks from the banks, and deposits of sediment build islands which disappear with the next floods.

We pass beneath thick layers of heavy clouds that hang so low I fear they might crush us. Our noisy engine sounds like an obscene intruder, but leaves only a trail of foam that vanishes without a trace.

As mile after mile slips away, a sense of isolation grips me.

Where the Amazon splits into the Ucayali, a major Amazon tributary, and the small Yarapa River, pink and gray dolphins leap by the side of the boat.

A lone fisherman stands in a canoe, his line in the water.

Trees and shrubs of muted greens and grayish browns rise along the high muddy banks. The coffee-colored water looks opaque. Fallen trees and branches litter the slopes. Moss and lichen cascade from the trees.

In front of a thatched roof hut high on the bank, naked children with distended bellies wave as we pass. An empty dugout, hewn from a single log, sways by the shore as a family bathes in the water.

When I travel I try to live from moment to moment: I try not to see too far ahead. Expectations only breed disappointment. Strange places often look different after only a day or two. I try not to draw conclusions, but the landscape gives me a hopeless feeling. Bare branches high above look forlorn. At the height of the dry season I see no flowers. Death and decay tumble through the living vegetation, strangling the fresh green growth.

It's hard for me to imagine that almost half of all the earth's species of plants, animals, and insects live in tropical rain forests. In South America, experts say there are probably ten to fifteen thousand species of flowering plants unknown to science, and two thousand unnamed fish; many species will probably have become extinct before they are discovered.

In the midst of this drab landscape, a dusty clearing marks the camp. High on the bank, a thatched roof watchtower on tall stilts looks ominous, as though the camp expects a surprise attack. The only sign of color comes from the plastic tub of the washerwoman on the raft, scrubbing brightly colored clothes.

On board, the men lazily rouse themselves from slumber and unload supplies. Insects buzz around our heads. A path of logs leads up the bank to the camp where several huts, half-hidden by banana trees, surround a circular, screened shack. I follow Paula and the men inside.

In the dim room, an emaciated figure, who turns out to be Andy, the other American volunteer, reluctantly raises himself from his hammock to shake my hand. His handshake feels limp. Andy is a bearded man with a pony tail, shirtless, barefoot, and tattoed.

He surprises me by suddenly leaping from his hammock. He disappears down a trail, returning with two ocelots, almost fullgrown. "These babies are almost ready to return to the jungle," he says, releasing the ropes around their necks. The way they growl and leap on Andy's legs, I believe him.

A tame capybara, almost as large as the cats, saunters out of the darkness under the dining hut. "The ocelots tried to kill her once," he says, "but she escaped into the river."

As rain begins to fall, I am shown to my hut. Large unscreened windows open out onto the jungle. I stare at the beautifully woven palm leaves of my thatched roof. Following the patterns, I become aware of creatures blending with the dried gray thatch. I watch a spider, almost the size of my hand, dangle from a thread. Lizards dart in and out of the woven fronds. More spiders crawl above my head.

I sit alone on my porch. The air has cooled, but the jungle looks bleak and forbidding in the rain. The tame capybara nuzzles my leg. Its coat feels rough and wet. I wish my guide Luis was here, but he's gone to buy Pepsi in a village. Even the volunteers are nowhere in sight.

Have I made a terrible mistake? I've never felt so cut off. The world feels so distant I wonder if I'll ever find my way back. I haven't felt this lonely since my first day at summer camp.

After dark, when I enter the dining hut, I feel Andy's presence before I see him in the quivering light of the lantern. He doesn't make me feel welcome. Even Paula's friendliness has vanished. She and Andy share a private language, excluding me and my guide, Luis, a pleasant-looking mestizo in his twenties who joins us for dinner. Luis looks longingly in the direction of the shack next to the kitchen where his buddies are eating. Their childlike laughter makes me want to join them, too.

I watch hordes of moths, mosquitoes, and unfamiliar insects fly around the lantern while giant cockroaches — some with wings — scurry over the table. Insects veil my dinner of rice, yucca, plaintains, and fish. I am quickly losing my appetite.

Paula leaves the table and returns with a squirming baby otter.

"She's only three weeks old. I have to feed her every four hours round the clock," she says.

"Waking up to feed her in the middle of the night must be rough," I say.

"Oh, I don't mind," Paula says, gazing at the animal like a mother looking at her newborn child.

Unlike Paula, I find its flattened head, broad muzzle, long body and short legs less than endearing. Though its eyes are still closed, its vocal cords seem fully developed.

"Does it always scream like that?" I ask.

"Ooh, she's upset. Baby is upset, isn't she?" Paula says to the otter, ignoring me.

While she and Andy discuss Baby's care, the creature's watery excrement leaks through her fingers onto the table. With toilet paper she cleans it up. I wonder why she has to do this at the dinner table.

Despite its shrill screams, she feeds it with an eye dropper.

When the otter is finally asleep, exhausted by its tantrums, there is silence at our table, a silence as heavy as the air. I glance at Luis who looks down at his plate. I'm sure he can't wait to escape.

Paula leaves the table at 8 PM, her bedtime, she says. Luis leaves the table soon after. Andy becomes suddenly talkative. He says he trained wild animals for movies and TV before he came here.

"For a Cadillac commercial, I trained a Bengal tiger to leap inside a Cadillac and exit from the other side," he says, picking at his rice. "I warned the client, I said, 'Man, this cat will rip apart the interior in less than five seconds!'" He looks at me intently. "But that jerk couldn't care less! He filmed that shot so many times I lost count of the Cadillacs destroyed. What a waste of money!" he says, in disgust.

"You must have made good money," I say.

"Yeah, but I hated working for those assholes. I would've gone crazy staying in California. When I came to Peru a year ago, I was looking for something to give my life meaning. The instant I saw this camp, I knew this was it. What Pepe is doing here to save the animals and the villages is really important work. I gave all my money to Pepe's project. I have only sixty-five dollars left," he says, grinning, exposing his rotting teeth. "I couldn't leave now even if I wanted to, but I'm happy here, the project is my life."

After my trip, I would learn that Andy has lung cancer. Doctors gave him two years to live.

In my peripheral vision, I've been aware of something large and black on the screen, but I haven't had the courage to take a good look until now.

"Is that tarantula inside or outside the screen?" I ask, trying to remain calm.

There is at least a half foot of open space between the edge of the screen and the unplaned planks of the wall so it hardly matters whether the tarantula is inside or outside.

"That's Mathilde, our mascot," Andy says. "She kills the roaches."

"Well, she's not doing a very good job!" I blurt out.

6

The gloom I felt yesterday has lifted. The sun has returned. The narrow river looks peaceful and silent this morning as I head toward a nearby village with Luis, in a canoe with an outboard motor. Several different kinds of kingfishers with glossy green or blue coats fly low near the banks. A black-collared hawk cries out from its perch high above.

Looking at the trees and shrubs and tendrils wound around the trunks, I begin to notice the variety of forms and colors. All the foliage is entwined. The roots of trees spread over the surface of the soil. From dead trees and roots rise the next generation. I feel as though I am witnessing a frozen moment in a violent struggle for survival until I become aware of the sighs of the forest and the tremors in the leaves.

Lacy filigrees of innumerable parasites clothe tall trunks in outlandish costumes. In the river, twisted, rotting trees like actors frozen in dramatic roles seem to pantomime tragedies.

From the boat I see pictures covering the wall of a thatched hut high on the bank. "What are those pictures?" I ask Luis.

"Naked women," he says, smiling. "In some huts they hang a picture of the Pope between pictures of naked women."

Hidden from the river by a steep, muddy bank, the settlement of Puerto Miguel, a dusty village of tattered huts around a soccer field, looks dreary and depressing. Here is squalor, without beauty or grace. What depresses me most at first glance is the slovenliness of the village and the traces of Western life. Aluminum pots and plastic bowls look strange on palm bark floors amid scraps of food, dirty pieces of cloth, and empty bottles of Pepsi. On the walls of the huts hang newspaper pictures of naked women.

A generation ago, Luis tells me, this was still a Cocama village. Recently, a few families of Mayorunas and one Jivaro family from Ecuador settled here. But now it is an insult to call them Indians.

Peruvians don't respect the Indian's self-sufficent jungle life: farming, hunting, and fishing for food is held in low esteem. To rise above their lower class status, the people of Puerto Miguel have adopted "civilized" values: they want what can be bought and sold for money.

The village lives off the fruits of the *aquaje* palm which are used to make popsicles in Iquitos.

"These fruits have female hormones," Luis says.

"What do you mean?" I ask, touching the small scaly *aquaje* fruit in his hand.

"If a man gives a woman these fruits, she won't be able to resist him," he says, smiling.

"How do you know?" I ask.

"Everybody knows that in Iquitos," he says, laughing.

As we walk down a dusty path along the soccer field, Luis asks if I am married. I shake my head, no.

"Were you ever married?" he asks.

"Yes, long ago," I reply.

"You are divorced?"

"Yes."

"Do you have children?"

"No."

"Not one?"

This village brings to mind a little story told by William James about a trip he made in the mountains of North Carolina where settlers had cleared parts of the forest and planted crops. He was disgusted by the charred stumps, the log cabins plastered with clay, the rail fences. In his eyes, they had ruined the forest. In time, however, he realized the settlers regarded these clearings as personal victories, the result of struggle and long hard work. He had been blind to their values; blind to everything that gave their lives meaning, as blind as they would have been to the virtues of his academic life in Cambridge.

Right now, I feel as blind as James felt in those mountains.

I feel sad that these ex-Cocama no longer value their native culture. For centuries the Cocama made beautiful pottery. To see it replaced by plastic and aluminum is painful to me. But perhaps I am just a romantic.

Many rural people in eastern Peru are descended from the Cocama Indians. In pre-Columbian times, they lived in communal huts along the larger rivers and controlled the region when the first Europeans discovered them on the Ucayali River in 1559. The Cocama were greatly feared as river pirates then. During the flood season, they plundered the villages of other tribes along the rivers, returning in the dry season with the spoils, and the heads of their enemies as prizes. The Cocama withstood colonial rule better than most tribes, though slave raids, smallpox, and measles reduced their numbers.

It seems such a pity that the only people who know how to live here in this environment without destroying it should so eagerly relinquish their way of life for the sake of "progress." But is it for progress? Or is it for survival? I recall Pepe saying that even here many animals have retreated deeper into the forest or disappeared completely, and fish are no longer as plentiful. Since the Amazon is a closed, interconnected system, I can easily imagine that destroying the forests elsewhere in the Amazon would have an impact here. Perhaps Puerto Miguel has no choice. Perhaps their old way of life would be impossible even if they wanted to continue it.

I can't help thinking, however, that the old knowledge of the forests and the rivers could be useful even now, if it is not already forgotten. Not all Indians are as eager as the Cocama to discard their traditions. The Shipibo, for example, choose selectively from our culture while retaining their identity as Indians. They still take pride in their past.

Behind the soccer field stands the primary school I saw in Pepe's snapshot. A large, unlikely billboard announces that Pepe's project built the school. Modest he's not.

Despite the school and the animals at the camp, my instincts tell me he's involved in something shady. I think the project is a front. For drugs perhaps? Or animal poaching? I hope I don't find out.

Across from the soccer field stands a two-story, thatched-roof shack in dirty shades of pink and blue, with an ornate wooden railing.

"That's the mayor's house," Luis says.

The other two-story shack belongs to the "professor" of the primary school. These two huts are barely raised off the ground.

"Don't those houses get flooded during the rainy season?" I ask.

"Only the first floors," he says. "During the rainy season they live upstairs."

Everyone we pass smiles at me and nods. I assume they are so friendly because most of the men who work at the camp live in this village.

The professor, a man about thirty-five, wearing spectacles, shakes my hand when Luis introduces us. Here is my chance to make contact with a leading citizen of Puerto Miguel, but I can't think of a thing to say. While he stands there, grinning at me, I am tongue-tied. I hadn't expected to feel shy. But I am slightly embarrassed walking around this village. I feel like a voyeur.

I count six gold teeth in the professor's mouth. Gold teeth are a sign of wealth. Nothing else in his appearance distinguishes him from the other men who all have shirttails hanging over baggy pants. He's also not the only one with gold teeth. Looking around, I'd say this was a wealthy village. The fillings, made by dentists in Iquitos, are often unnecessary. Despite their gold fillings every adult I see is missing several teeth. One man with wedge-shaped teeth, filed Cocama-style, startles me when he smiles.

Most of the people here look Mongolian, with broad flat faces, high cheekbones, almond-shaped eyes, and straight black hair. Hunting parties from Asia may have crossed a land bridge where the Bering Strait is now, and traveled south, some, all the way down to the Amazonian lowland jungle which they first reached about twelve thousand years ago. They survived as hunters and gatherers, living in small nomadic bands, but as they adapted to the jungle, their numbers grew, and they developed into chiefdoms with independent villages.

In this village, I look for vestiges of the past. Besides crude wooden beds — typical Cocama beds — with slats across the bottom, and handwrought canoe paddles, there is little to suggest their tribal life, though they once were considered a great nation.

Luis shows me a jawbone with piranha teeth that is used as scissors. The old sewing machines they use are the same as the ones in Belén. Among the paraphernalia on floors and crude wood tables, rubber boots, sandles, straw hats, hatchets, and machetes lie in disarray. Clothing is carelessly strewn over roof beams. Chickens wander through the ashes of last night's cooking fires. I think to myself, this village could use some good brooms.

The one true vestige of tribal life that still exists are the shamans who consult with the spirits of the rivers and the forests to cure illness, find stolen possessions, or forecast future events. But Pepe told me belief in the shamans is weakening, and villagers often ask him for pills.

One of the shamans was a cook at the camp, Luis tells me, but Pepe fired him for drunkenness. I wonder if this was the cook who tried to crawl into bed with Paula.

Leaving the village, we pass small plots of yucca and banana plants, and the only beauty spot of Puerto Miguel: a patch of earth where fallen blossoms from a leafy tree cover the ground like hot pink dust.

Climbing the steep bank of a smaller settlement called Libertad, Luis says, "You will like this village better." But I'm not so sure. I'm looking at three panting women dragging a heavy dugout up the slope. At the top, several men are idly standing, watching them.

I hear loud music even before we enter the village. Evidently, everyone has radios so they can keep in touch with distant members of their families. In Iquitos, relatives even broadcast coded messages, informing their aunts or uncles or cousins of changes in market prices.

The music and the fresh, green fields of rice stretching for miles along the banks lift my spirits, though the huts are as dirty as those of Puerto Miguel.

The camp is shrouded in darkness by the time we return from

the village.

I can count on the company of Andy and Paula to lower my spirits at dinner. But at least I'm not alone with them: Luis has joined us again.

I walk outside after dinner with Luis beside me. The sky frightens me at first with its brilliance. I have never seen so many stars gleaming with such intensity. They seem magnified. Weighed down by its dazzling burdens, the sky seems low enough to touch the tree tops. Venus shimmers. The Milky Way looks like an ocean of muted beams slithering across the sky.

Luis' closeness has escaped my attention till now. His face touches mine as he tries to guide my eyes toward the Southern Cross. I follow his finger pointing straight up to clusters of stars, but his warm breath distracts me. His other arm is around my shoulder.

Suddenly I feel uneasy, alone in the jungle at night with this guide I barely know. Perhaps my suspicions are wrong. Perhaps his intentions are innocent. By jungle standards I'm old enough to be his mother. I'm not sure what to do.

I feel relieved when he suggests we walk to the river where it will be easier to see the sky. But when he takes my hand to lead me in the dark, like a reflex my hand jerks away. In the dark I look at his face. I see a mixture of hurt and childlike surprise. I wish I could undo what I have done. I feel angry at myself. The wariness I brought from home has no place here. I want to say something, tell him I'm sorry, but still I'm not quite sure. Have I made a mistake? Have I misinterpreted his motives?

7

Paula was nearly in tears this morning when her Walkman broke. She said she'd have to wait a month to fix it in Iquitos. "The paid help get more time off than the volunteers," she said bitterly, in a rare moment of anger at Pepe. She claims she hasn't received mail for two months though she knows her mother has sent letters and packages to the office in Iquitos.

Paula's outburst surprised me. Usually the volunteers talk about Pepe as though he were their guru. A few minutes later, Andy surprised me, too: when I offered them a mystery I finished reading, he practically tore it from my hand.

Only the Peruvians seem content here, though they make me uneasy. They watch me when they think that I'm not looking. They grin and snicker among themselves, and sneak around the huts without a sound.

In the dining hut this morning, two of them hid in hammocks in the small space behind the bar. I didn't think there was room for one hammock much less two, until they arose from their siestas or whatever they were doing.

I wish I could relate as well to people here as I relate to the jungle. Luis has been afraid to touch me since I pulled my hand away. Now I need his help on the trail. I'm having a hard time, but he doesn't seem to get the hint when I joke with him about my clumsiness. We are speaking Spanish now. He's teaching me new words.

I gather my courage. "I'm sorry about last night," I say to him.

He looks at me, puzzled.

Perhaps this is just my fantasy that he's afraid to touch me now, but I have to finish what I started.

"I felt frightened for a moment when you took my hand," I say to him, embarrassed.

"You were frightened of me?" he asks, surprised.

"Yes, I know it was silly," I say, though I'm still not sure it was silly, but he seems harmless in daylight.

He laughs.

I guess he thinks I'm just a crazy gringa, but at least I've cleared the air.

The forest is still cool and very quiet. I hear only the sound of our feet crunching leaves and the collapse of roots, vines, and branches severed by Luis' machete.

Everywhere I see life piled upon life. This profusion and variety would be impossible without the constant dampness and warmth. I see climbers and epiphytes, air plants which grow on other plants and need no contact with the soil. The jungle looks chaotic because the climbers and epiphytes obscure the layers of trees. A miraculous order, however, based on the struggle to survive, underlies this apparent chaos.

Through gaps in the foliage I can see the tallest trees rise above the rest, but they are few. Their trunks, like the giant cedar in front of me, rise unbroken by branches until they reach the canopy. The canopy, including fruit trees and palms, reminds me of a man with thinning hair. The trees are just thick enough to block the light. Below this layer are smaller trees.

Very little sunlight filters through the canopy, so the ground is relatively free of plants except for shrubs, seedlings, and young trees. Here, the huge buttressed roots of the ceiba or silkcotton tree flare like skirts, and the palm's stilt roots keep it anchored in the shallow soil.

The upper layers are the best place for life because they get more sun and rain. Competition for light is fierce among plants and animals.

Most animals are nocturnal and live in the canopy, but each layer is host to different species of animals, birds, and insects. Each species has a special place. Mosquitoes that carry malaria, for example, live in the main layer. Only when the forest is cleared do the mosquitoes descend and prey on people.

In the soft mud, Luis points out two giant *ponerine* ants, almost $1^1/2$ inches long. Their stings can cause high fever and shock. Some say four stings at once can be fatal. He finds their nest by the roots of a ceiba tree. As he digs his machete into the nest, dozens flee in great confusion.

I am careful not to touch anything, for there are other insects to watch out for beside the *ponerine* ants. Some insects, among them caterpillars, hornets, beetles, and millipedes, release poisons when disturbed, which cause excruciating pain.

The more insects Luis shows me, the more I realize that the stillness is an illusion. Under fallen seeds, pods, fruit and fungus, on rotting logs, in the air, on trunks and branches and roots and vines and leaves, insects abound!

He points out a butterfly with transparent wings resting on a leaf. The wings cast no shadow. How many other creatures are here which my untrained eyes can't see?

Some insects have protective coloring. There are butterflies that look like leaves and bark, stick insects indistinguishable from twigs, lizards and moths patterned like lichen, tree frogs that change color, insects with outgrowths far larger than their bodies which look like thorns, fungi, buds, or leaves.

There are also insects that mimic other insects. A predator will avoid eating an edible butterfly if it looks like a poisonous or inedible one. Wasps and flies have mimics. The more the mimic looks like an insect that is dangerous or distasteful to a predator, the more chance the mimic has for survival. Even the insects that I see may not be what I think they are.

When a tree dies and falls to earth, termites quickly break down the wood. Their nests, made from forest debris glued with the insects' saliva, protrude like huge boils from forks in the trees. It's amazing that these creatures which are completely blind can build such nests.

A milky resin oozes from the wound Luis makes in the bark of a rubber tree.

I step over a giant white fungus, a foot high perhaps, which resembles the mushroom cloud of an atomic attack in miniature.

I pocket seeds and pods — some as big as fruit — that Luis picks up to show me.

All my senses feel alive. I watch Luis move through the forest with ease. He knows this forest well. Still, he seems excited to show me an insect, a plant, or a tree.

Light filters through gaps overhead spotlighting the curve of a branch, the pattern of veins on a leaf. My head swims in an element richer than air, a steamy substance boiling with life. In the forest I forget myself. I'm no longer the woman from New York.

There are even more restrictions here than there were in my mother's house, but as I follow Luis along the trail, I feel the freedom I felt on my first trip. I feel the freedom I dreamt of long ago. I am still Rima, the jungle girl in *Green Mansions,* but this time I am living my dream.

What a contrast there is between the freedom I feel on my hikes with Luis, and the constraints I feel around camp. It's not just the gloomy meals with the volunteers that bring me down. I feel trapped within the confines of this jungle clearing. There is nowhere to go on my own. I am stopped by the forest, the river, the bugs.

Paying constant attention tires me. In the outhouse, in the shower, in my hut, something is always flying, crawling, or hiding in the shadows. I wish the jungle were more like the vacant lots where I played as a child. I could go home after playing. If only there were one safe, screened place away from the heat and the bugs.

The first night I made the mistake of putting my kerosene lantern near my bed. The lantern attracted scores of visitors: moths, mosquitoes, bees, and giant wasps which live near my hut in the cecropia tree where the long sac-like nests of oropendolas hang suspended. The birds choose trees with wasp nests to protect them. I wish these wasps would choose a different tree. While waiting for the wasps to fly off, I discovered a strange nocturnal bug with green iridescent eyes among the spiders on the wall.

After dinner, Luis, who has eaten with his cronies tonight, waits at the door of the dining hut to take me out on the river to see alligator-like caimans. Any excuse to stay up past our 8:30 bedtime is good enough for me. Except for my face and hands, my clothes protect me from the insects which are particularly vicious after dark.

The river seems strangely silent at night despite the cries of rats, croaking frogs, and cicadas. The shriek of a bird sounds like an echo in a tunnel. Luis and a local boy paddle noiselessly along the timber-strewn bank while I sit between them in the small dugout. Leaping fish ripple the water, and birds rustle through the leaves, but these sounds only heighten my sensation of floating through a void. Even the sky seems to have vanished, and left in its place, a great emptiness where unhinged stars glimmer. The eyes of nocturnal birds glow in the dark. In the beam of Luis' flashlight, the tangle of dead trees and floating debris lining the shore look like unearthly stage sets. Suddenly a pair of eyes like red-hot coals appear on the bank. Excited, Luis creeps ashore with the boy behind him. In the bleached-out landscape of his flashlight beam, a baby ocelot — a rare sight — stands like a phantom, frozen in the spotlight until it suddenly bounds back into the forest. Luis is so excited he forgets I am here until I nervously call out in the darkness. My voice seems to come from some far-off region. From a distance Luis and the boy seem like actors in a ghostly play, and for a second I imagine I am here alone. Reluctantly, Luis returns to the boat, but not before he spots a giant otter — an endangered species — fleeing between the trees. When he turns the flashlight to the shallow water by the dug-out, I glimpse the slithering form of an electric eel caught by the beam. Luis is still excited as we head back to camp, but I feel as though I am dreaming.

I'm glad I left my jungle adventure books at home. Harry A. Frank's tales about his journey on foot from Ecuador to Argentina early in this century seem too real here as I squash stray mosquitoes that have managed to get under my mosquito net. Sleeping under this net brings to mind cocoons, coffins, wombs, even cobwebs. Depending on my mood, I feel sheltered and safe, or I feel trapped, with little room to move because everything I need for the night surrounds me in my bed: my flashlight, my watch, my journal, a pen, a novel, a water flask, a mixture of rubbing alcohol and oil for bites, and long pants and a sweatshirt for late night strolls to the outhouse.

Lying here, I think about the books I read by women — anthropologists, missionaries, wives of oil men and engineers. The most amusing account of domestic life I found in an old *National Geographic*; it was written by an oil man's wife and titled "I Kept House In A Jungle."

But the most interesting woman I discovered was Maria Sibylla Merian, a German-born artist and scientist who journeyed to the Surinam rainforest at the age of fifty-two in 1699, more than a century before the great naturalists, von Humboldt and Darwin. After two years in the interior where she became ill with a fever, she returned to Amsterdam with a wealth of wildlife paintings, notes, and nearly one hundred insect specimens new to science.

My thoughts are rudely interrupted by the wind. Suddenly, the trees outside my hut seem made of elastic as they bend and sway. Thunder sounds like the sky cracking open. Lightning flashes through the camp, followed by torrential rain. I lie awake, watching, listening, hoping I won't have to make a late night trip to the outhouse where I was warned there might be snakes even on the clearest of nights. In sudden blazes of light I see through the filmy netting, trees fighting to keep their ground. I hear branches break against the walls of my hut. The sound of wind, rain, and thunder, however, is soothing to me. This rampage is nature's release. Silence, not sound, makes me uneasy here. That strange night silence brings to mind whispering voices of wandering Cocama spirits perhaps, but in this storm nothing wanders about. I pass the night in a drowsy state until I fall asleep near dawn.

I dream that the roaches, the snakes, the spiders have become more than I can bear. I need to take a breather. I fly to Lima, but instead, I arrive in New York. What time can I return? I ask the ticket seller, but she sells only train tickets. I can't go back! I am filled with remorse.

When I awaken, I am thrilled to hear the rasping calls of oropendolas. They sound like heavy gates swinging on rusty hinges. Their calls are my reveille here. I listen to a medley of bird songs: weird ringing monotones, series of chants, low notes, high notes, rapid notes, some many times repeated, others that sound like whistles, chimes, or bells. How thankful I am that my leaving was only a dream!

8

The men at this camp behave like boys, sly boys. To them, everything is a game. The other day I watched as three of them, giggling like school boys, chased the terrified chicken that was to be our lunch. Waving their machetes, they surrounded her, but they were laughing so hard it took them an hour to calm down enough to kill her.

Luis is ill this morning so Héctor will guide me instead. I would never guess that Héctor is the camp manager. He looks dull-witted except for his leering smile. He's been lurking in corners, watching me since I arrived.

"We will go and see the dolphins," he says in Spanish, smiling. I follow him with some trepidation to the motorized canoe. Despite his lechery he is childlike. But he is not a child, I remind myself.

"Where are you from?" Héctor asks. "Are you married? Do you have children? How old are you?"

Héctor says he is thirty-five and unmarried. The unmarried part is unlikely since men wed at fifteen or sixteen here.

Along the river, Héctor stops to pick up a woman from Puerto Miguel. She wears two skirts and two blouses and carries a basket of laundry. Héctor flirts with her, forgetting me completely until he drops her off along the bank.

Near a long sandbank, freshwater dolphins leap from the water. One pink dolphin is among the ten or so we see. Pink dolphins are more primitive than the gray ones. They are slower, larger, more solitary, and have long narrow snouts.

Dolphins flourish because they are sacred here. Legends say they are very fond of young girls, and can disguise themselves as humans. If a young girl becomes pregnant by a dolphin, she suffers no disgrace.

We watch their gymnastics. I am less than enthused, though Héctor seems to be enjoying himself. I miss Luis. He seems more honest than the others. If he were here now I'd feel relaxed, but with Héctor I feel slightly uneasy. Heading back, even the jungle on the banks seems closed and impenetrable.

Paula told me Pepe had sent word that he was coming today. At camp, the supply boat has arrived, but Pepe isn't on board, and neither is the money he owes me for the delay in Iquitos. Three new visitors have arrived, however: a young French couple who speak no Spanish, and hardly any English, and an American man in his forties named Ray.

"Howdy," Ray says to me in a Southern drawl as he enters the dining hut and takes a look around. He has an enormous toothy grin. He wears shorts and combat boots. After he's surveyed the premises, I see a sardonic look in his eyes. He says, laughing, "I like that open space around the room between the screen and the wall. At least nothing as big as a jaguar can squeeze through, but I bet there's heavy insect traffic at night."

"In the daytime, too," I say, laughing. I point out Mathilde, the tarantula, inside on the screen.

Ray shakes his head. He's a wise guy, but he's sure to enliven dismal meals with Andy and Paula.

"I'm a contractor," Ray says, "so I notice how things are built. Actually, contracting is only a sideline. Since I retired from school teaching, I've become a chicken farmer. But I'm in Peru to build an orphanage in Iquitos."

"How did that happen?" I ask.

"Well, I built an orphanage some years back in a jungle swamp in Costa Rica. This group of businessmen in Tennessee with money to burn approached me when they decided to do a good deed. I just checked out the site. I'm on my way back to the States now to hire a crew to bring down here. If I hire Peruvians, the work will take forever. Bringing my own men will cut costs, and we'll finish the job in three months.

"But I don't think these businessmen would be too thrilled," he says, smirking, "if they knew they were building an orphanage for children of unwed mothers. I wonder how many couples legally marry in Iquitos."

"I have no idea," I say to him.

"I tried to call my wife in Tennessee to tell her I'd be home a few days late, but all the lines were down in Iquitos," he says, looking serious. "I hope she doesn't worry. But I thought I'd check out the jungle while I'm here."

The French couple look perplexed; they watch us with wide eyes.

"I haven't been able to find out much about Alain and Marie-Juliette. They're both doctors who've been traveling around Peru," Ray says. "That's all I could figure out."

I'm glad Luis feels better after lunch. Ray's wise cracks about New York grow tiresome.

At Puerto Miguel a three-day fiesta is underway. The men are drunk on *aquadiente,* a powerful homemade sugercane rum. From the mayor's porch, boys in soccer uniforms cheer for several men playing a drunken version of soccer.

"Hell, I didn't have to come to the jungle to see this," Ray drawls. He looks out over the river. "Have you been to Catalan?" he asks me.

"No," I reply. "Paula, one of the volunteers at camp, warned me not to go. The mosquitoes are unbelievable, she said. And the snakes! You sleep in an open hut near the ground, and climb trails that are steep and slippery. I think I'll stick to the sights around here."

"Well, I want to see Catalan," he says. "That's where all the animals are. I think you should go."

"I don't think I'm ready for Catalan," I tell him. "It sounds like more than I can handle."

I follow Luis and Héctor, who is guiding the others, down a trail of mud, liquified by the overnight rains. On and on we trudge. I wonder if this trail ever ends. We finally stop by a *chacra,* a patch of forest cut and burned for farming.

Traditionally, yucca is planted amid the burnt stumps and blackened logs. Burning provides a layer of nutrient rich ash.

"This is a shortcut," Luis says.

When I take a good look at the *chacra,* I wish we were back on the trail. We climb over huge trees sprawled on the ground in all directions. Thorns and vines scratch our arms. Charred wood spikes rise from blackened thickets. Spiders and ants in dizzying profusion claim the rotting timbers. It's a miracle that none of us are bitten or stung. I trip over tangled branches, and catch my foot in a crevice between burned roots. What's the point of this? I wonder, as Luis and Ray extricate my foot. "We're almost there," Luis says, to placate me, though I can't see the end of the *chacra*.

"There!" Ray says. Between trees in the distance, I glimpse the clusters of giant lily pads I saw in Pepe's snapshot, floating on the glasslike surface of a lake.

Marching between thorny branches and sharp spine-covered palms, we finally reach the slimy bank, edged with weeds. Pepe wasn't lying about their size: each lily pad is five or six feet across, with delicate red and white flowers, but I'm not sure seeing them was worth this effort.

The serenity of the lake seems unreal.

I look behind me for a moment at the *chacra*. "Hiking at Catalan is probably as bad as this," I say to Ray.

"Catalan is all wilderness!" he says, laughing. "There's nobody there to cut and burn trees."

Luis is standing very close to me. His arm brushes mine.

"In Brazil," he says, "babies float on the lily pads, but here in Peru, the babies sink."

"Why?" I ask.

He shrugs.

Halfway around the lake, Luis and Héctor lead us up a steep bank, dotted with plants whose serrated edges can cut like a knife. At the top I see a grove of huge strangler fig trees. The sight is unearthly. With the profusion of hanging roots, they look like multi-armed monsters.

I can't tell where one tree ends and another begins. The gnarled gray roots twist in tortuous shapes, and reach out like great devourers in all directions. With their rounded knobs, they look like the enormous bones and joints of dinosaurs rearranged in grotesque patterns and grafted together, the work of a mastermind with a fearsome imagination and a streak of cruelty.

Stranglers begin life as epiphytes, or air plants, high in the trees, and send down roots into the earth for nourishment. Gradually, the roots encircle the host trees which support them. Stranglers seem to crush their hosts with their melded tentacles wrapped tight, but in truth, they kill their hosts by stealing the light and water as their crowns spread out in the canopy. When the host is dead, it stands like an upright corpse, trapped inside the strangler till it rots.

Even these trees, these killers, protect other forms of life. Lizards and ants, bees and wasps live in the nooks, crannies, and hollows. At night, bats fly from their roosts, and scorpions hunt for crickets and cockroaches. The figs attract troops of monkeys, flocks of parrots, and beautifully plumed macaws. The fruits which fall to earth feed rodents and peccary, agoutis and pacas.

Everything is connected in this forest. Everything has its place. It boggles the mind to imagine how this master plan evolved.

I feel awed as we march back in the brief twilight. But I don't feel awed for long. The trail demands all my attention. The holes, ruts, and deep puddles that were hard enough to skirt in daylight, are impossible to avoid in the dark. I slip and fall.

Sitting in that primal ooze, I feel a moment of abandon: I am a child playing in mud. How much better to feel like a child than to be one! This is the freedom that comes with age. I am laughing as Luis and Ray pick me up. Covered with rich brown slime, I am laughing all the way back to the camp.

The cold water feels refreshing as I shower in the darkness under a spray of stars while large spiders crawl along the walls, and lizards dart across the floor. Only the mosquitoes are a nuisance.

I think of the family I saw today in a sinking canoe who laughed while bailing water with a bowl. I feel as though a door has sprung open inside me. I will go to Catalan, I tell myself.

9

An early morning haze accompanies our departure to Catalan, the remote camp about thirty miles upriver in the high jungle. Crammed with camping gear, there is barely room in the motorized canoe for Ray, the French couple, the guides, the cook, three local boys, and myself.

Traveling upstream, the canoe slides under arches formed by huge fallen trees, festooned with moss and lichen. We glide over a carpet of tangled hyacinth; the thick, shiny leaves and delicate purple flowers, however, are not as innocent as they appear. By absorbing the nutrients released by decaying trees, the weeds kill both plants and fish. The hyacinth spread over the surface, blocking sunlight from the water, often becoming a breeding ground for malaria.

Luis points out a group of bats suspended upside down in a gutted log protruding from the hyacinth. Their motionless forms blend with the wood. But as we pass, about a dozen shrilly-squeaking bats fly from their hiding place, their wings beating the air.

Eight cormorants keep pace with the boat, diving for fish about twenty yards ahead.

Millions of bugs gush like a fountain from a hollow log.

On steep muddy banks, webs of exposed roots reach down to the shallow water. Flat-crowned ceibas rise high above the rest.

Beards of gray moss spill from branches. A throng of hanging roots look like rain. Bromeliads dangle on the limbs of fallen trees.

The forest is denser, the trees taller, the birds more numerous and varied as we travel upstream. Here, I can understand why early European settlers thought the soil was so fertile until they harvested their first mediocre crops of maize and manioc. They didn't realize that the fertility of the forest is in the vegetation, not in the soil. Few nutrients reach the thin layer of soil, which only allows for shallow roots. The Amazon forest is a closed system in which the same nutrients are used over and over.

In the old days, Indian farmers moved their villages every eight or ten years. Their cut and burned fields were small and short-lived, and the forest replenished their plots.

When a large area is continually cleared or burned, the forest doesn't grow back. Every patch of Amazon forest is unique, so the destruction of even a small area means the extinction of many forms of life.

Great Blue herons sail over the water. A dome of cloudless sky replaces the early morning haze. The sun and heat make me drowsy. Lying on a mattress between Ray and the French couple, I feel as content as a baby rocked in a cradle.

I wonder why the French couple whisper, no one here understands their language.

At the stern, a local boy steers with the six foot throttle of the outboard while the guides direct him from the prow. They judge the position of dangerous logs underwater by subtle shifts in the current. Every so often — like now! — I am jolted into consciousness when the boat scrapes a rotting tree along the bottom. We are stuck fast until the guides push the boat from the log with their paddles.

"Did you know there are falcons in Manhattan which nest on tall buildings?" Ray says to me.

"No, I didn't," I reply.

"I bet you don't know half the birds in New York City," he says, grinning, trying to provoke me.

"You're right, I don't," I say.

Just then Héctor points out a pair of noisy toucans high in a tree. A few minutes later, we see two capuchin monkeys swinging from branches.

With wings of iridescent saphire, Morpho butterflies as big as birds flutter along the banks.

While the boy refuels, I watch a flurry of bright red spiders spin their webs across every rubbery hyacinth leaf in the tangled patch near shore.

Further on, a shimmering stream juts like a black sleeve from the Yarapa River. I wonder if I am seeing things as I watch the black channel and the chocolate brown Yarapa flow side by side without mingling.

Dyed by rotting vegetation, black rivers flow from the north. Brown rivers like the Yarapa, with silt from the Andean highlands, flow from the west. I can't imagine what this black channel is doing here: the nearest black river on a map, the Rio Negro, is miles away.

Announcing our arrival at Catalan, seven pairs of blue and yellow macaws with long tail feathers fly high across the river like airborn jewels. In contrast to this dazzling display, the grim campsite makes me wish I had listened to Paula.

Catalan is nothing more than a decrepit unwalled hut, perched on a high bank, in what was once a clearing. Abandoned and forlorn in this vast expanse of jungle, Catalan is the loneliest place I've ever seen.

Escorted by convoys of moths and butterflies, we climb the steep bank. Standing at the top, I look in horror at the vibrating wall of insects surrounding the hut. Among the unfamiliar species, I see mosquitoes, horseflies, bees, hornets, wasps, dragonflies, moths. I am frozen to the spot when suddenly, clouds of tiny black flies attack us, each one no bigger than a dot. I feel little stabs of pain all over. They even find their way into my socks. I leap about like someone with St. Vitus Dance, and try to wave them away. They leave tiny, blood red marks on my skin.

Following the guides, we charge through the haze of insects, throw down our knapsacks in the hut, hurriedly change into swim suits and run back to the river, the tiny black flies still in hot pursuit.

Jumping into the river, I feel the most exquisite relief! The thick soupy water feels like heaven. The presence of piranhas seems a minor threat. The thought of encountering electric eels, stingrays, alligators and anacondas doesn't bother me at all. Even the possible presence of the toothpick-sized *candiru*, a parasitic fish that must be surgically removed once its spines open out like a fan in the orifices of the human body, can't dim my happiness at escaping from those tiny black flies!

But my happiness lasts only a moment. Before I know it, the swift current is pulling me downstream. Using all my strength, I swim back to the muddy bank.

Ray, who dove from a high point up ahead, floats quickly past, as motionless as a log. I hope we will see him again.

In our absence, the men have made a fire to smoke-out the insects. Ray, the last to return, is short of breath and ghostly white.

"That's some river!" he says, grinning. "I wasn't sure I'd make it back."

"Neither was I," I say.

"How long do you think it would've taken those guys to notice I was missing?" he says, glancing at the Peruvians who are giggling again while a caldron of rice cooks on the fire. "They would notice very fast if *you* were missing," Ray says to me.

"I'm not so sure," I say.

"Luis and Héctor would notice. Believe me," Ray says.

While the men play at preparing lunch — they're in no hurry — Ray and I lie in the shade on moldy mattresses. I glance uneasily at a very active hornet nest, directly overhead in the low roof as Ray tells me about his pregnant daughter who married a hillbilly.

I can't help thinking this is an unlikely place for this conversation, as green iridescent flies zoom past my ears and butterflies drink the sweat from our skins.

When at last lunch is served, insects rally round our plates of fish, rice, and yucca. Chasing them from the food becomes more tiresome than sharing my plate.

The black flies must be sleeping off their meals. We were probably the best banquet they ever had.

A while later, dark clouds fill the sky, and heavy rain falls. An Amazon shower is not like a cloudburst at home: one inch of rain can fall in thirty minutes, up to forty times more water than in a shower in the American Northeast.

Walls of rain wrap us snugly in the shelter. Catalan no longer feels strange. Everything seems transformed. I feel a rightness about being here; I feel as though I am in exactly the right place at the right time. Everything fits, even Ray's chatter.

We head upriver in the canoe when the rain stops, hoping to

spot more birds. But the sky seems to be covered by a sheet of dull gray metal. The air feels like a solid block around me. Not a leaf stirs; the trees are caught in the viselike grip of the air. The forest seems to wait for some cataclysmic event to shake it loose. Deep within the forest, birds hidden in their dark nests or perched on branches far from view must also be waiting. Even the insects are silent.

About forty minutes from camp the boat sputters along the river when suddenly, thunder, like great steel plates crashing through the sky's metal floor, sends its sound through the pit of my stomach.

Luis and Héctor strip to their underpants, and stash their dry clothes under the prow just before a deluge of windswept rain engulfs us.

Lightning etches the sudden darkness, and bathes the jungle in momentary flashes of eerie yellow light. Through veils of rain I see Luis' bare back illuminated by lightning: his skin glows with an unearthly light.

Dimly outlined, the jungle sways and trembles in fitful dances; a grand coupling of the earth and sky takes place. Bare branches like open arms yield to the downpour.

Flocks of shrieking birds soar in alarm as the boat heads back to Catalan. Somewhere a mad conductor leads an atonal symphony of wind racing wildly through the trees. When the wind pauses, the strange, muffled cries of animals pierce the darkness.

The banks are nothing but dark blurs when suddenly, carried by the water, a deafening sound like an explosion, makes my heart stop for a second. A chunk of the bank has collapsed into the swelling river. I feel the boat roll and lurch like a drunken sailor. The landslide has created a chain of waves which has set off more landslides along the banks.

Filled with trees and debris, the waves bounce back and forth between the shores, throwing the boat one way, then another.

Wind lashes my skin. My teeth chatter. I am numb with cold and fright. I wonder if this is the end, as a large piece of driftwood strikes the side of the boat, tipping it dangerously in the water. As rain pours from the sky like a second sea let loose from the clouds, the canoe fills up. But the motor is still running. I start to pray and hold on tight to the edge as the boat weaves between the fast-moving trees. In the darkness, I keep my blurry eyes pinned on Luis' bare back; somehow, it makes me feel safe.

In Luis' flashlight beam, the hut looks like a ghostly gray presence in the downpour. I am shaking as Luis drags me up the bank of liquified mud.

I crawl under my airless mosquito net onto the soggy mattress. I am wet, cold, hungry, and plastered with mud. I am also laughing! Ray is laughing too. He just told me the men tied the canoe to a paddle stuck in mud!

"We may have to swim back," he says, hardly able to get the words out he is laughing so hard.

A while later, thrashing around in his bed beside me, he groans, "It's too early to sleep."

I am also wide awake. I hear the Peruvians laughing at the other end of the hut. For a moment, I see Luis' smooth skin in that storm when I close my eyes.

The cramped quarters don't faze the French couple who are moaning in the mosquito net beside me. The bark floor bounces. Their heavy rhythmic breathing almost puts me to sleep until they tumble against my mosquito net.

The storm is directly overhead. Lightning flashes as thunder rips the sky. The jungle smells rancid in the still air.

"Maybe you should sleep in my net," Ray says, laughing. "At least you won't get trampled."

"I am almost in your net now," I point out. I've moved to the far side of my narrow bed. Only mesh walls divide me from Ray.

The French couple have enormous stamina. I resign myself to a sleepless night.

"Are you awake?" Ray whispers every few minutes.

I laugh in response.

10

This morning my hair feels as matted as moss on the trees. My skin is coated with mud and sweat. The Peruvians look upset when I use bottled drinking water to wash, but I don't care.

The sky is overcast. Two of the boys chop down small trees for a fire. I wonder how they will start a fire with wet wood. I wonder if we will ever eat breakfast. We haven't eaten since yesterday's lunch.

Ray looks relieved when he sees the boat below, filled with water, but still tied to that paddle in mud.

I see Marie-Juliette has traded her blue stretch-pants for ones with leopard spots, and changed the long diaphanous scarf around her neck for one of a diffent color. She has the oddest jungle wardrobe I've yet seen. I hadn't thought about making a fashion statement when I packed my T-shirts and jeans.

After washing, I feel human again, and join Luis who is seated on a log reading the Spanish-English dictionary I loaned him. The antics of the French couple last night stirred my fantasies about Luis, but I have no intention of acting them out. There is, however, a chemistry between us, though I've never been attracted to a man with three gold teeth before.

"What are you reading?" I ask him in Spanish.

"I don't know how to spell English words," he says. "I learned to speak English by listening to the radio. I learned to speak German that way, too."

"Don't they teach English at school?" I ask.

"Yes, but I didn't go to college. I had to leave school to help my family."

"Do you want to go to college?" I ask him.

"Yes," Luis says, "but I don't have the money or the time. Even if I got a scholarship my job would interfere."

"How many people are in your family?" I ask. I realize how little I know about him. I'm not even sure where he lives.

"I have three married brothers and three married sisters. They live with their children in my parent's house."

"They live in Iquitos?"

"In Belén," he replies.

"In Belén?" I repeat, surprised. "Do you live there, too?"

"Yes, I live with my parents."

I never imagined Luis living in that slum. "And are you married?" I ask.

"No," he says.

Is he really unmarried at twenty-five? I wonder, but I change the subject.

"Is it dangerous to live in Belén?"

"Not in the daytime. But at night there are robbers who hide in the shadows and grab you. They beat you with clubs, then steal your money."

"Has it ever happened to you?"

"No," Luis replies, "I am very careful."

I never thought of Luis having a life outside the jungle.

"Which do you like better," I ask, "the jungle or the city?"

"I like both," he says. His three gold teeth glitter when he smiles.

I notice a tiny shack I've not seen before behind the hut.

"What's that?" I ask.

"A chicken coop," he says.

The shack brings to mind the Colombian traders, imprisoned like animals in tiny, filthy cages by Arana's men, who gained control of their Indian laborers during the rubber boom.

The Peruvians cast sly looks and snicker in our direction as the cook hands us plates with fish, rice, and yucca — again.

Luis, looking at the chicken coop, says, "Last year I took a group of Americans here. Their leader was a fat, black, bossy woman who ordered everyone around. One night two men in the group got so angry at the woman, they carried her kicking and screaming to the chicken coop, and swore they'd make her sleep there unless she shut her mouth. She was very quiet after that," he says, smiling.

"Who were those people?" I ask.

"Members of some cult. I don't remember the name, but they came to take *ayahuasca*, the drug the Indians use to go into a trance. Pepe hired a local shaman to give them the drug," he says, smirking.

"You must think Americans are crazy."

"Germans, too," he says, laughing.

A hike is not exactly what I'm in the mood for, but everyone else wants to see the animals so I stumble along behind them on the trail, which feels like a sponge beneath my feet. Hanging roots and tangled webs of woody vines emerge from shadows like hallucinations of a mad sculptor. Unlike the land downriver, this hilly country requires a lot more stamina.

I've never been a very good hiker. My fear gets in the way. Here I am fortunate to have help from Luis and Ray.

On the trees, Luis points out high water marks well above our heads. It's amazing to imagine fish swimming through the branches of the trees during the rainy season, feeding on fruits and leaves, dispersing seeds like birds.

In the mud we see fresh tracks of a tapir, the largest animal in the forest.

Plants with long, sticky leaves grab at my pants. When Luis bends down to touch one of them, the plant closes around his finger. "That's how they trap insects," he says.

I am fascinated by the streams of leafcutter ants on a decomposing log. Their trails look like two-lane highways seen from the air. In one direction, they return to cut leaves with their long mandibles, while in the other, they carry disk-shaped bits of green many times their size to their underground nests, which may be half a mile away. Some nests cover a quarter of an acre and house more than a million ants.

Soldier ants guard the mounds that protect their dwellings. Their jaws, sometimes used as sutures or stitches by the natives, clasp so tightly they won't let go even if their heads are severed.

In their subterranean nests, with intricate passageways and chambers, the leaves are used to grow fungus to feed the ant larvae. This fungus may be the world's oldest cultivated plant. Leafcutters, however, can strip a grove of young trees overnight and are a menace to farmers.

The naturalist William Beebe once dropped a leaf on their trail, and watched one ant haul it out of the way, though the leaf was more than one-hundred-fifty times its size. The effort would have equaled that of a man carrying eleven tons for fifty yards.

We pass a nest of ants with black bodies and white heads. Luis warns us to be careful. Their stings are very painful, he says.

Further along, we approach a tree that seems draped in layers of filmy white gauze. "Social spiders," Luis says.

"There must be thousands!" I say in astonishment. When I look closely, I can see the little spiders inside the delicate webs which seem to have no end. In places the thick layers look solid. The tree looks ghostlike beneath its white veils.

Even though Luis and Ray have to hold my hands crossing a slender log over a stream, the trail seems easier now. I trudge through the mud with more confidence.

I am feeling good about myself when suddenly I feel a stab of pain. I clutch my leg and cry out. I see several giant ants scurrying across the trail. Luis pulls a four-inch spider off my sopping jeans. But he says, "The spider didn't bite you."

We continue along the trail, down, up, then down again, skirting slimy black pools and vines braided like Rapunzel's hair. I am waiting to see what reaction I will have to a bite by a giant ant. But a while later I realize I have forgotten about the bite. The trail requires all my attention.

When Luis calls out, "Army ants!" I envision a swarm miles wide advancing through the jungle. I remember this image from a film. This stream of ants, however, is less than a foot wide and moves in an untidy column across the trail. Some make bridges of their bodies so others can pass. They look confused to me, tumbling about, some running backwards, some colliding, others breaking out of line. They look so unstable I wonder that they build nests at night with their bodies clinging together in chains.

Relying on their sense of smell and taste, they raid the forest floor or the trees, collecting debris and all the small creatures in their path which they break down into food for their queen.

Human breath will whet their appetites for flesh, but their stings, while painful, are not dangerous.

When one of the boys up ahead lops off some large palm fronds overhanging the trail, a loud buzzing fills the forest. Irate wasps, their nest disturbed by his machete, fill the air. Luis tells us to stay very still. He takes my hand very slowly. "Follow me, but be very careful," he says.

"I'm scared," I tell him.

"So am I," he says.

I hold my breath as we inch our way forward through the haze of wasps. Sometimes tens of thousands of these yellowish wasps live in one colony. I hope this is a small one.

When we are safe, I return to that relaxed yet attentive frame of mind where I am open to whatever happens next. I am often in this frame of mind on our hikes in the jungle. I lose track of the hours, but I am aware of every moment. Instead of fear, I feel elation.

Looking around me, I see the cupped leaves of a fern holding rainwater; I see a world of tiny living things swimming in the pool at the base of a bromeliad; a hanging root steals food from that pool.

I see tracks of caterpillars in chewed-up leaves, vines with little feet like suction cups, smooth wood behind peeling strips of bark, green buds on a shoot between dying leaves.

I see all the opposing qualities of life locked together in an inextricable embrace. I see weakness and strength, softness and hardness, roughness and smoothness, darkness and light. These vines and leaves and branches show me more possibilities for life than I ever imagined. The Amazon is my model. I see birth and growth and renewal. I see how what is old and dead contributes to the living. Like the forest reaching out for light, I am reaching out, embracing all I see and feel.

11

Home? Did I hear myself say "home" when referring to the camp downriver? Yes, I just asked Luis: "When are we going home?" I guess human beings can adjust to anything. I would probably start calling Catalan home, too, if we were to stay a few days more, but we won't.

The others are disappointed because we haven't seen animals in the last two days, aside from a few monkeys, but I'm not disappointed at all. I even got a good night's sleep, though my mattress still feels like a sponge. I suspect the French couple wore themselves out on their marathon the night of the storm.

I never imagined that I would miss the outhouse at the base camp downriver. Getting up in the middle of the night makes me yearn for even the simplest of facilities. But I've been very lucky here. On my nightly forays, I haven't met any snakes or tarantulas or scorpions, just the usual assortment of bugs.

This morning I am up before daybreak with the Peruvians. I understand now why they awaken so early. The air is cool and free of insects! This is the only time of day to do any work.

Our motley group is heading upriver to fish for our next meal.

The shores are alive with birds. A flock of screeching parakeets with pointed tails cross the river and disappear in the trees. The canoe, which fortunately didn't fare as badly in the storm as I feared, turns off on a quiet stream. I mistake the mottled bark of half-submerged trees for the rough scales on the backs of caimans.

Branches shooting upward from the water sway in rhythm with the gently flowing current.

In a dark, shady cove, the boy stops the motor. The silence is disturbed only by birds' wings flapping against the trees and the occasional calls of kingfishers.

I hadn't realized until now that we are going to fish for piranhas. I didn't even know they were edible, but Luis says I've already eaten them twice for dinner at the camp downriver. There are lots of piranhas there, too, he assures me.

"You mean the water where you and the men bathe every day is filled with piranhas?" I ask.

"Yes," Luis says, "but the piranhas by the camp don't attack."

Fishing in the Amazon is not like fishing in the States. Luis and Héctor hand us bamboo poles with hooks attached to lengths of fishing wire. We bait the hooks with bits of catfish. Then we beat the water with our poles for several minutes. We all feel terribly silly, but the fish are attracted to the turbulence which they mistake for fruit falling from the trees.

Marie-Juliette is first to feel a tug on her line. We duck as she swings the line into the boat, an orange-bellied piranha struggling on her hook. Its incredibly powerful snapping jaws expose a mouthful of razor-sharp, wedge-shaped teeth like those of a shark. Removing the fish from the hook is tricky business. In a split second a piranha can snap off a finger. Like a razor cut, a bite is painless at the moment it occurs.

Héctor dislodges the fish and bangs its head against the boat. Less than a foot long, the piranha flaps about the dank bottom of the canoe.

More often than not, the piranhas escape with the bait, but we still catch one every few minutes. The fish have no aversion to eating their own, so when we use up the catfish bait, Luis chops up the smallest piranhas for our hooks.

We grow accustomed to dodging each flying piranha as it sails on a line above our heads. None of us is adept at hoisting in the line without a reel.

Within three minutes a school of hungry piranhas can strip a capybara to the bone. Sometimes, however, even chunks of fresh meat or animal blood will cause no reaction. There are no less than twenty species, some more ravenous than others. They are most dangerous in the dry season when trapped in slow water, but no one really knows what triggers their attacks. Even piranhas of the same species may behave differently.

The piranhas we are eating for lunch are quite tasty, but hundreds of small bones are a nuisance. The insects like the fish as much as I do. I bet these insects will miss us when we're gone.

Twilight only lasts a quarter of an hour in the Amazon, but those minutes are not to be missed. The river is already tinged with purple when we return to camp. In the sky, a crimson streak spreads like an ink blot. The men bathe at this time every day. The ones who didn't accompany us to Catalan are already in the river, with the laundrywoman's little boys. Their idea of bathing is different from ours. Laughing, they push each other off the raft, then return and douse each other with bowls of water. Watching this game, I realize these men, who live so completely in the present, use every opportunity to enjoy themselves. I think everyone gravitates toward good times, but rarely have I seen people enjoy themselves with such abandon.

Since I've been here, I feel I've become more like them, or more like what I imagine them to be. I've been able to get out from underneath my thoughts. What draws me to them now is the direct way they experience life.

The laundrywoman has come to bathe in the river. She looks sullen, her mouth curves down. On the raft, apart from the men, she scrubs her long hair, her face, her arms, and her shapeless dress, as though the fabric is a second skin. What is making her unhappy? I wonder. I realize I know nothing about a woman's place in this camp of men as I watch a pulsing, orange sun slip behind the silhouettes of trees, while fish leap from the river like slivers of silver.

Paula and Andy are amazed that I enjoyed Catalan despite the landslide and the rains.

"We didn't think a woman from New York could survive Catalan," Paula says, half-joking.

With Ray here, the atmosphere in the dining hut has changed, though the French couple have the same look of incomprehension they've worn since they arrived.

Despite the French couple, who barely exist for me, I feel connected to this unlikely group who have become my family here.

"It's a pity you didn't see the animals," Andy says.

"When were you last at Catalan?" I ask him.

"Last year," he says.

I wonder if perhaps Pepe has already emptied Catalan of wildlife. Who would know? There are no policemen here. Perhaps he returns token animals to the jungle to keep himself looking clean.

Months after my trip, an American scientist would accuse him of large-scale poaching, but he offered no evidence.

Ray tells Andy how the men tied the canoe to a paddle stuck in mud during the storm.

"It doesn't surprise me," Andy says. "Nothing they do could surprise me. There was a time when the supply boat broke down and we didn't get supplies for two weeks. Every day I checked the food rations. I warned them we were running out. But they just smiled. Only when the last tins were empty, the last bananas gone, would they so much as fish in the river. I never saw such lazy people," he says, disgusted.

"They don't see things the way we do," I say on their behalf.

"They sure as hell don't!" Andy says. "I wouldn't trust any of them from here to the river."

I'm in no mood to argue. To change the subject, I ask, "Is Héctor married? He told me he wasn't."

Andy and Paula laugh.

"Héctor has a wife and children in Puerto Miguel," Andy says.

"What about Luis?" I ask.

Glancing at each other, they barely suppress their smiles.

"Luis isn't legally married," Andy says, "but he has a wife and a little girl. He lives with his wife's family in Belén."

I feel very disappointed. I didn't think Luis would lie to me.

Andy says, "The men who live in town usually have wives in the jungle, too. Sex is very casual around here. When they don't have women, they sleep with each other."

Ray finds this terribly amusing.

"How do you know?" I challenge Andy. "You don't even speak Spanish."

"I have eyes! I can see what goes on," he says.

I think about the laundrywoman. A few days ago, I saw the men playing with her little boys amid the soiled sheets and dirty clothes on the porch of her hut. Crouched on the floor, I saw her laughing, presenting a different face from the sour one I saw when she was working.

"Who's the father of the laundrywoman's children?" I ask.

"Each child has a different father," Andy says. "But all the men love those kids. That's their only redeeming quality. Did you notice?" he says, turning to Paula. "She's pregnant again."

Over coffee, Andy tells us he was bitten by a fer-de-lance last year, one of the most deadly snakes in the jungle.

"A shaman brought me back to life," he says.

"What did the shaman do?" I ask, wondering if this was the shaman/cook who crawled into bed with Paula.

"After he cut open the wound and sucked the venom out, he chanted and poured herbal potions down my throat. That's what the men say. I was in a coma."

Paula has black circles under her eyes. The shrieking baby otter probably kept her up again all night.

I ask her why she hasn't eaten anything.

"I've been sick," she says, sighing. "On every trip to Iquitos, I see the doctor. I'm sure I have parasites, but nothing he prescribes seems to help."

"Why don't you go back on the next supply boat and see another doctor?" I ask.

But she shakes her head, no, and lets out a long sigh.

"First thing I'm going to do when I get home is send you two a care package," Ray says, grinning.

Before we left for Catalan, they had shown him the moldy books on the bar they claimed to know by heart.

While Ray makes a list, I notice the tarantula is missing from her usual spot on the screen.

"Where's Mathilde?" I ask nervously.

"Mathilde died," Andy says.

"How?" I ask.

"The pesticide must have killed her. She probably ate some *cucarachas* after the hut was sprayed."

"There don't seem to be any missing," I say, glancing at the giant cockroaches running about the table.

Ray's loud laughter echoes in the night.

12

After Catalan, my hut feels like a palace. Sleeping on a dry mattress seems the height of luxury. Before dozing off last night, I remember hearing laughter from the dining hut. Andy and Ray stayed up late, drinking. This morning after breakfast, Ray is leaving on the supply boat which finally arrived yesterday, without Pepe. I think Pepe keeps the men in line this way. They never know when he will surprise them.

"If you write any articles about this place, let me know," Ray says, grinning, handing me his address, as he boards the supply boat with the French couple.

Watching the boat speed downriver, I feel suddenly as alone as I felt the day I arrived. The same light rain is falling. The camp looks as dismal as it looked that first afternoon. I glance behind me at the drab jungle hugging the clearing. The days ahead seem suddenly long and uncertain. Am I growing tired of the jungle so soon?

I am startled to see Luis standing beside me. I hadn't heard him approach. I'd almost forgotten him.

"There's a difficult trail upriver," Luis says, "that leads to an Indian village. Pepe lets very few people see this village. Do you want to try?"

"Are they really Indians?" I ask.

"Yes, Mayorunas. Untouched. Pepe takes scientists to see them sometimes, but almost no one else. He doesn't like to disturb them."

"So why am I being honored?" I ask.

"You are writing an article for Pepe. He told me."

I doze in the motorized canoe as we head upstream with one of the local boys who works at the camp.

When I awaken over an hour later, I ask Luis, "How much farther is this trail?"

"It's still far," he says, as he motions the boy to steer clear of a large piece of driftwood floating toward us.

I have no idea whether we're still on the Yarapa River, but I'm too drowsy to care.

The drizzle has stopped by the time we climb a muddy bank.

"Where's the trail?" I ask, looking round me. All I see is water, with mounds of mud. There were heavy rains again last night.

The trees are thinner here than the dense forest at Catalan which held the water. Luis notches the trees as we trudge through the soaked forest. He and the boy push rotting logs across the deepest pouches of water, and help me across.

I think of old cartoons of chivalrous men placing handkerchiefs over puddles so ladies in high heels won't wet their dainty feet.

My feet, however, are anything but dainty. Despite their gallant efforts, I slide into deep, soupy pockets. I am embarrassed by my clumsiness.

Where the logs are too heavy to move, they chop down small trees to form makeshift bridges while I listen to the gurgling sound of water, streaming in all directions. A rancid smell fills the air. The matted forest seems to sink under the weight of so much rain.

Each time I slip I become more afraid.

"Oh no!" I cry out, as we near a ditch perhaps twenty feet deep and just as wide, spanned by a skinny log that reminds me of a tightrope.

"That's impossible! There's no way in the world I can cross that!" I say to Luis.

"I will show you," he says, unconcerned.

Luis and the boy cut down two skinny trees, to use as staffs. Like aerialists they cross the log, one foot in front of the other, balancing on the staffs which reach to the bottom of the pit. When they are midway, I hear the log crack.

"Luis!" I cry out.

"It's O.K." he replies.

The boy waits on the other side as Luis comes back to help me.

"Just put your arms around my waist," he says.

I do that, and step out on the log, but I jump back in fear. The boy returns. Despite my protests, each one places a hand beneath my armpit, and the three of us walk sideways. They steady themselves with their staffs. The skinny log groans under our weight, and sags in the middle. I lurch forward, but they hold me fast. I feel weak when my feet touch the ground. I hope the Mayorunas are worth this.

The jungle is even swampier here, with more deep pockets. On and on we trudge until Luis stops so suddenly I almost bump into him. His arm shoots out to stop me.

"What is it?" I whisper.

I follow his eyes to a huge slithering form a few feet from us. I can just make out the yellow and brown markings. I know exactly what I am looking at before Luis says a word. We stand perfectly still while the anaconda decides what to do. I think of the anaconda I saw in the zoo. I wish there were bars between me and this one. Slowly, it backs up and moves away.

"They come out after the rains," Luis says, when it has disappeared.

"Is this forest ever dry?" I ask.

"No, but I didn't think it would be like this," he says.

It's impossible to see where I am stepping. Up ahead, it looks even worse. No wonder few people visit the Mayorunas. It looks to me like they'll be safe from *civilizados* for quite a while.

Alone, the boy goes on ahead to see if he can find a way around the water.

Luis and I stand on a mound of mud. The trees around us look black. Luis looks up at the overcast sky through the wet leaves. For the first time since I've known him, he looks worried.

"Do you think it will rain again?" I ask, nervously.

"I don't know," he says.

I feel as though we've been standing here forever when Luis cups his hands over his mouth: a strange bird call rolls into the forest. We wait, hearing only the rustle of leaves and water streaming nearby.

The stillness is getting to me. I need to talk, to make contact.

"Did Pepe teach you about the forests?" I ask. He couldn't learn all this living in Belén.

"Oh no," he says. "I grew up in the jungle. I only came to Belén a few years ago."

Luis cups his hands and calls out again, but the sound, swallowed by the still air, makes the forest seem even more silent than before.

He tries one more time. We hear a faint echo. The echoes grow louder until the boy appears between the trees.

"There's no way around the water," the boy says solemnly.

I'm disappointed to have come all this way for nothing, but I've been dreading the hike back more than I've been looking forward to my visit with the Mayorunas.

Nothing looks familiar to me as we head back. The fallen timbers and deep cavities don't look like the ones we passed before. I begin to feel drugged by the strangeness, the silence. Luis hurries me along until we reach the terrible pit — a landmark I remember too well. Their hands in my armpits before I can complain, they almost carry me across the skinny log.

I sleep all the way back to camp, awakening only as night, like a great eyelid closing over the river, traps me like a speck of dust.

After dinner, I'm too restless to lie in bed so I return to the dining hut to write in my journal. The hut is empty now except for the bugs. The swarms of insects outside keep me from walking down to the river. It's no wonder jungle people go to bed early. There's nothing else to do.

I've grown used to the din of the cicadas and frogs at night, but the creaking hinges on the screen door startle me. Luis is standing there in the doorway, bare-chested after a shower; his hair is dripping wet. Héctor is close behind him. "Hello," we call out in the near darkness. I return to my writing, but I feel uneasy. I look up to see the two men, barefoot, walking noiselessly across the room to lie in the hammocks behind me. The air is suddenly filled with tension. What's going on here? I feel as though their eyes are boring holes in my back. I tell myself I'm getting worked up over nothing. This is Luis. I know Luis. But this Luis doesn't seem like the one I know. When I turn to look at them, I see their black eyes staring out at me like cats' eyes in the darkness. They are slowly rocking in their hammocks, their hands behind their heads. Should I leave? No. I have as much right to be here as they do. Why should I let them force me from the hut? I try to continue writing, but I'm too aware of them to concentrate. Could I be in danger? No, no, this is some kind of macho game. Isn't it?

My thoughts are suddenly interrupted by Luis.

"You write a lot," he says. "Maybe you write too much."

"Maybe," I reply, not knowing what else to say.

The words hang in the air like damp clothes on a line. I am waiting to hear more, but he says nothing.

Is there some rule I don't know? Perhaps a woman isn't supposed to sit alone here at night. Perhaps my being here has given them the wrong idea.

Without turning around, I'm aware of Héctor rising from the hammock. He walks to the screen door and opens it slowly. "Goodnight," he says, smiling slyly.

I hear the crunch of moth wings burning in the flame of the lantern as I try once more to return to my journal.

I feel Luis rising from the hammock though I haven't heard a sound. The silence is as loud as a scream. He is standing a few feet behind me.

Suddenly, I turn to face him, surprising myself. "What are you doing?" I say.

He is standing there smiling at me, not saying a word. He is deciding something. I can almost see the little wheels spinning in his brain. I hold my breath.

Slowly, he heads toward the door. "*Hasta mañana*," he says, softly, before the screen door shuts.

In front of my hut, I stand for a moment, looking up at the patch of sky between the banana trees. Insects sound like millions of tiny saws that never stop. Trapped in darkness, birds shriek across this vast echo chamber of night. I brush mosquitoes from my face and listen to the plaintive cry of a bird that sounds lost in space. The forest shudders as a sudden breeze strokes its branches. I take my kerosene lantern in from the porch.

13

On the river, the sky is a hard, flat blue. In the bright light, the forest seems as two-dimensional as Henri Rousseau's jungle scenes. Rousseau never saw the jungle. His paintings were inspired by tropical plants in the botanical gardens of Paris. His painting, *The Dream*, was my favorite work of art when I was a child. I spent hours in front of it. *The Dream* portrays a naked woman lying on a sofa in a jungle of exotic plants, giant lillies, ferns, fruit, and birds. A dark figure plays the flute while animals peep out from thick foliage. In that painting I saw my dream: that jungle was paradise.

The jungle I am seeing now reminds me of that paradise; the forms are so clear every detail is visible.

No particular feature stands out in the jungle. The jungle is an accumulation of details, a multitude of relationships that reveal themselves slowly to the eye. Both time and patience are required to decipher this language of forms. Discovering the jungle is discovering secrets in that vast grayish green wall.

I always need to catch hold of some small part which moves me in order to comprehend the whole. I agree with the French philosopher, Gaston Bachelard, who wrote, "The cleverer I am at miniaturizing the world, the better I possess it." Small things keep me from feeling overwhelmed. Perhaps it is odd to be drawn to things that seem to be without consequence when taken alone. But nothing exists alone here. The discovery of one relationship yields a hundred more, and that hundred, a thousand, and so on. The picture of a whole takes shape slowly in my mind like a tapestry, first examined thread by thread.

Colored by the sky, the Ucayali River is deep blue. The river flows from the south, filtering white sandy country. Against the wind, in a dugout, Luis and the boy paddle vigorously in a wide arc toward a long, white beach. A mile back, against the jungle, stand the thatched houses of San José.

The pure white sand is broken by narrow channels where sandpipers feed. In the stark light, the beach looks unreal. The whiteness, the emptiness make me feel as though the world has disappeared.

Luis says this is a good place to swim, but I haven't brought my suit. He looks disappointed when I say I won't swim in my underwear. He says that everyone swims in their underwear. For a moment I hesitate, the water looks so inviting, but then I remember last night.

As Luis walks out into the river, he beats the surface of the water with his palms. I hope he's not trying to attract piranhas.

"Why are you doing that?" I ask, from the shore.

"Stingrays!" he yells back. "If there are stingrays on the bottom, they will go away."

It's odd that I should think of Coney Island here — the antithesis of this beach. I loved Coney Island when I was a child. My father used to take me there. We kept our excursions a secret from my mother who was horrified by even the thought of Coney Island. A few years ago, I went there out of curiosity. I was nearly as horrified as my mother would have been. In that sea of humanity, it was a wonder no one was crushed.

I say to Luis in Spanish, "If this beach was in New York, there wouldn't be a foot of space without people."

"Yes?" he says, surprised.

"And there would be very loud radios playing different songs and garbage all over the sand."

"Yes?" he says, again. "Are the people on that beach black?"

"Black and brown and white."

"There are many Latinos in New York?"

"Many."

"But they live separately, away from the whites?"

"Some do," I reply.

As we walk along the beach toward the village, I see where water has evaporated in narrow streams, the sand has dried and cracked in beautiful linear patterns that resemble the designs on Shipibo pots.

On the high bank above the beach, the path to the village is bordered by orchards of fragrant fruit trees and gardens of plants and herbs. Facing the river, the huts line the path like a string of beads. I feel an air of serenity, a peacefulness here. San José is also a Cocama village, detribalized in the last few years; but the atmosphere is very different from that of Puerto Miguel. Even the huts are clean.

Walking from hut to hut, the women welcome Luis and the boy

whose grandmother lives in this village. The children giggle when they see me, but their mothers barely look in my direction.

In her mother's arms, one little girl, however, stares at me in wide-eyed terror before she bursts into tears. Luis laughs and says, "She's never seen a gringa before." Though her mother tries to calm her, the child's sobs grow wilder, her eyes pinned on me while she pulls at her mother's hair. "Your green eyes scare her," Luis says, still laughing.

The little girl makes me feel like a spectacle. I feel even more of a spectacle when I almost fall from the steep steps to the hut of the boy's grandmother. Two of his cousins, seated on the porch, can hardly control their laughter. Nevertheless, I admire the babies in their laps, hoping for a sign of friendliness. They ask Luis if I have children. When he tells them "no", they look at me, surprised. I see a touch of pity in their faces.

I'm beginning to feel like a freak. I feel large and ungainly here, though I'm slim and five-foot-three. The girls, however, in conversation with Luis — a little king reclining in his hammock — forget all about me.

The boy's grandmother gives Luis a large clamshell as a present when we leave. As we continue along the path without the boy, Luis gives me half his shell. Maybe he can see I feel dejected.

"What will you use the shell for?" I ask him in Spanish.

"For eating," he says.

I was wondering where the men are. Luis is pulling me quickly past the bar, set back from the path, almost in the forest, but I get a good look at the drunken men crowding the windows, waving and shouting as we pass. I had thought they might be fishing.

There are still plenty of fish in the Ucayali River, though manatees and large river turtles, which were once the Cocama's main diet, are rare if not extinct.

Game is also scarce, but their rotated fields provide them with manioc and corn and other crops; and, of course, they have fruit trees, wild plants, nuts, and seeds which they gather from the forest.

In a small garden, Luis points out plants used to cure various ailments. Different parts of one shrub are used to cure children's diarrhea and intestinal worms.

Two children mash manioc in a wooden mortar the way their ancestors must have done centuries ago.

Luis joins a mother and her daughter, sorting beans on a mat. In no time, they are all howling with laughter. When I bend down and help them, the women glance at me, amused. I am almost sorry I bothered, but I'd feel even sillier just standing there, waiting for Luis.

Afterwards, I ask him what was so funny.

"We were talking about rising prices," he says.

"What's funny about that?" I ask, but he shrugs and says nothing more.

I am delighted when an elderly couple invite us inside their hut while they strip the husks from ears of corn that rise in a pyramid halfway to the roof. The husks form another pyramid almost as high as the corn. Their daughter, whose small son sits in her grandmother's lap, brings us a large bowl of water to drink which I decline. I carry bottled water.

"Where is her husband?" I ask Luis, wondering if he was one of the men at the bar.

"She has no husband," he says.

"Do many women have children without husbands?" I ask.

"Marriage is not so important here," he says.

The old couple smile at me and make me feel welcome. The old man asks where I am from. "Very rich city," he says in Spanish when I tell him.

I am amazed to see newspaper pictures of the cast of *Dynasty* on the wall behind me.

"How do they know about *Dynasty?*" I ask Luis.

"Everyone knows about *Dynasty,*" he says. He asks me to repeat the name. He wants to pronounce it correctly.

Until now, San José seemed close in spirit to the way I imagined an old Cocama village would be.

"Have you ever seen television?" I ask Luis.

"Yes," he says, "in Iquitos."

I remind myself that jungle people aren't as isolated as they seem. The networks of rivers keep them in touch with one another, and in touch with Iquitos, though during the rainy season they don't travel as much.

But what do they understand when they see the cast of *Dynasty?* Does this old man think I live like those cardboard characters on the screen?

Heading back through the village, I notice a hut with a new corrugated metal roof, set back from the path.

"The rain must sound very loud pounding on that roof," I say to Luis.

"But it's stronger and lasts longer than thatch," he says. "More people would have metal roofs if nails were not so expensive."

The boy joins us as we pass his grandmother's hut.

"Tell me about New York," Luis says.

"What do you want to know?"

"How much does your house cost?"

"Four hundred dollars a month. My house is very cheap," I say, "because I've lived there a long time."

Luis calculates the amount in his head, converting dollars into *inti,* the Peruvian currency which is about as stable as mercury. The boy, who seems as lethargic as ever, suddenly perks up. "How much?" he asks Luis.

When Luis tells him, I try to register his reaction, but his face looks as blank as before.

"How many rooms do you have?" Luis asks.

"One big room with a kitchen and a bathroom."

"Only one room?" Luis looks at me in amazement.

"Yes."

"There are many people living in your house?"

"Just me."

"Do you live in a very tall building?"

"No. My building has only three floors."

"But there are people living in very tall buildings?"

"Yes."

Luis shakes his head and laughs. "New York is dangerous?"

"No, not if you're careful. But it's more dangerous than Iquitos."

"More dangerous than Belén?"

"I would think so."

"You can walk alone at night in New York?"

"In certain places. Some parts are safer than others."

"Is it safe where you live?"

"Yes."

"I want to go to New York some day," Luis says.

"I don't think you'd like it," I say to him.

"Why?"

"Everything is so big, and there are so many people. And everyone thinks too much about money."

He says, laughing, "People here think about money all the time, but they don't have any. I think I would like New York."

As Luis and I walk back to the boat over the pure white sand, he is telling me about a film he saw in Iquitos called *Cannibal Holocaust*. I realize something has changed between us. I am no longer the rich gringa. He is no longer the guide. There is an ease in the way we are together that didn't exist before. We are friends, enjoying each other's company.

I feel as though I am seeing him for the first time in full dimension. In my fantasies, he has been the focus of my desire. In reality, he has been my bridge to this world. But I haven't seen him apart from my needs until now.

The boy has wandered off somewhere. We retrace our steps to find him. Reluctantly, he follows us back to the boat.

14

I don't think Luis is sitting here at dinner with me to insure himself of a big tip when I leave. But he must be aware, though neither of us has mentioned it, that my stay is almost over. I feel touched that Luis has chosen my company tonight. After all, a meal with me means a meal with the volunteers. I know he can't stand Andy and Paula. He's told me so. He barely says a word during dinner. I try to help him feel at ease, but he seems embarrassed and keeps his eyes on his plate. For once I'm glad to see Héctor enter the dining hut. Luis looks relieved when Héctor suggests a game of gin rummy with Andy.

While the three men play, I lie in a hammock and write in my journal. Luis feels braver with Héctor nearby and approaches me when they take a break.

"What do you write in that book?" he asks.

"Everything we do each day," I tell him.

"Why?" he asks.

"Because I want to remember everything."

He laughs.

I still have fantasies about Luis. I'm tempted to act them out just before I leave, but that's just another fantasy. I know I'll do no such thing. Still, the thought is there.

In the last couple of days, I've grown more restless. The camp feels even smaller. I hate to admit it, but I feel bored between my outings with Luis. I feel confined. Sometimes, I'm tempted to take a trail and go off by myself, but that would be foolhardy.

As I drift off to sleep, I am thinking about Luis.

Am I dreaming? I feel groggy. What's that I just heard? There it is again. It sounds like a heavy thump. I am wide awake now in the dark. I am listening. I hear insects and frogs.

There it is again! Oh God! Something is jumping onto one of the wooden posts supporting my mosquito net! I feel my body grow rigid. I am afraid to move a muscle. I wish I could see what it is. Calm down, I tell myself. My eyes are growing accustomed to the darkness. I can make out a valley in the mesh above my feet. A creature is sitting on that post. I see the shadow of its body in the net. What is it?

I hear a low purring.

Oh my God! Don't panic, I tell myself. I can't cry out, I might scare it. Then it will plunge into my bed. My mind is racing. Has one of the ocelots escaped? Could this be a jaguar? Are there jaguars in this forest? No, no, jaguars live far away from people. Maybe this one has strayed, lost its way.

Whatever it is, it's moving again! It's turning on that post. Oh, it's jumping over my bed! It's landed on the post behind my head.

It's right above me! I'm afraid to breathe.

I hear a thump. I think it landed on the floor. It's walking around on the floor.

I don't hear anything now. Is it gone? I think it's gone.

This morning I wake up in a sweat. I have one night left before I leave. Do I have to worry about wild animals my last night here?

Luis has checked the ocelot cages, but the animals are where they belong. He shrugs. He doesn't know what it was. He's never seen a jaguar in this forest.

"But you've seen an ocelot!" I say.

"Yes," he says, "but ocelots are rare."

"Well, what else purrs in this jungle?" I ask him.

My enthusiasm is dampened as we head upriver with the boy. I heard from Andy that Lake Cumeseba, our destination, is the most beautiful spot in this jungle, but I keep imagining ocelots and jaguars behind every tree.

As we approach the large, still lake, reflections in the water create a double world of vine-laden trees and shores rimmed with hyacinth.

I've never seen so many birds! They move in strange orbits through the trees and over the water, filling the sky with layers of sound and sparks of color. A pair of black caracaras pierce the air with their cries. A yellow-winged cacique flies from its pendulous nest. With its gooselike call, a horned screamer the size of a small turkey rises from a patch of hyacinth, its black wings flapping, a long spike curving forward on its forehead.

"Are you going back to Iquitos tomorrow?" I ask Luis.

"Yes," he says, but his attention is focused on the lake. "There are *paiche* here," he says, handing me a fishing pole, "and fish we can sell to acquariums in Iquitos."

In the dry season, many fish migrate and breed in upstream

shallows and backwaters.

Luis wrestles a large catfish from the water. His pole bends and twists as the fish struggles on the line. The boy spears a fish with sinister teeth. A large fish bites my hook but slips away. My line snags on driftwood. I lose interest in fishing. I let the sun's hot rays dissolve my thoughts. My mind as liquid as the lake, I drift into a half-sleep and dream:

The lake is contained by a great bowl buried in the earth. The bowl is filled to the rim. In the center of the lake, I lie in the boat, Luis and the boy beside me. A half-sphere of clear blue sky completes the circle. I see the veins in the diaphanous, violet-tinged wings of a dragonfly as it flutters and loops before me. Beyond this peaceful world, the sky darkens, gray clouds bleed, and rain falls, but not a drop touches this tiny universe which begins to move, slowly upward, then around the earth, past angry whirling seas filled with whitecaps, past islands in green oceans of coral, past cities enveloped in yellow haze, past craggy, snow-capped peaks. Here, in this tiny sphere, this still center, nothing can be lost, not even a dragonfly.

When I awaken, the thought of leaving Luis and leaving these forests and rivers saddens me. I had been looking forward to returning to Yarinacocha, the lake where I stayed on my first trip. In the beginning, I had thought of this camp as my training ground: I would learn about the jungle and prepare myself for my trips to Shipibo villages. But this camp has been more than a training ground.

Hearing about the small viper back at camp that Andy killed last night on the path to the outhouse doesn't make me feel better about leaving.

"We'll see a lot more snakes around here with the rainy season coming," Andy says.

After dinner Luis enters the dining hut. "You're not writing tonight?" he says, smiling.

"No, the next time I write will be in Iquitos. Are you glad to be going home?" I ask him.

"Oh, yes, I am very tired," he says.

"Did I make you tired?" I ask.

"Yes," he says, laughing. "Most tourists need more rest."

"I can rest at home," I say, laughing, but tears are not far off.

The other men enter the hut. Usually they slink into the shadows, but this time they surround the table, watching us. There is more I want to say to him, but the men make me feel self-conscious.

In the morning, after an undisturbed sleep, Luis appears with the laundrywoman's oldest son, a child of ten or so. "We have time for a little walk," he says. "The men are working on the supply boat."

In the shadowy darkness of the forest, the child runs between us, picking up little twigs and bits of leaves that he presses into my hands as gifts of goodbye.

With Luis' help, I have seen my dream in the world. When I enter the forest, I enter myself: I enter my dream and I see myself inside out. Leaving will not sever my connection here. I carry this jungle inside me, and this jungle holds part of my history now. I came alive here. I gave myself the freedom to explore. And I gave myself the thrill of discovery.

When I was a child, my world was safe as long as I followed the rules, but my world offered no joy, no surprises. There wasn't room to grow. It was a world bounded by "no's" that I've carried with me ever since. Here, I let some of them go.

Boarding the supply boat, I try to hold on to this expansiveness I feel, but my mind fills with mundane details instead. I sit alone at the prow while the men crowd together in back.

Up ahead, I see a wide expanse of water. We are approaching the

Amazon. I look back one last time at the narrow channel of the Yarapa, overhung with brownish trees. Everyone is asleep now except for the motorman and me. I feel as though I am emerging from a dark tunnel, a place of stillness. I feel a brooding presence release its grip. Sadness passes through me like a sudden pain and is gone.

The boat plows through the open water at full speed. The wind takes my breath away. The boat leaps in the air, then crashes down on the water, sending clouds of spray on deck. Who would think this relic could move so fast? Sand whirls on the banks, and lines of little trees sway in the wind.

My first glimpse of Iquitos fills me with excitement. Iquitos could be Paris or Rome! I see the familiar skyscraper, its singed shell rising over the roofs. I see the church steeple in the Plaza de Armas, and farther away, the huts of Belén, jutting out on the water.

Belén wouldn't have shocked me if I had seen the jungle first. In Belén, the people live the way they live in the jungle, but there is no jungle in Bélen, and there are no amenities of city life. They live in a floating twilight zone on the river.

Luis carries my duffel up the steep, rickety stairs of the dock near Pepe's office. By the crumbling balustrade on the promenade, a dozen men around Luis' age make remarks as I pass. How different Luis seems from them.

Streets have never looked so astonishing! I see cars, rickshaws, taxis, bicycles speeding past.

While Pepe is holding court with some of the men in his tiny loft, I wait with Luis, who stands across from me at the table. I am trying to control my tears. "What will you do now?" I ask, handing him a tip which he gratefully accepts.

"I will sleep for a week!" he says, smiling.

Pepe calls. I wipe my eyes and climb the tiny spiral staircase.

Wearing a Mickey Mouse T-shirt, Pepe leans back in his chair. Smiling, he says, "I hear you had a good time."

"Wonderful!" I tell him. "And Luis was a wonderful guide!"

"That's why I chose him for you," Pepe says in his oiliest voice. "I am sorry I didn't get to the jungle. I miss the jungle very much. But I had so much work, and now I have terrible pains in my legs." His lips curl down in a dramatic show of suffering and he places his stubby hand over his heart. "The doctor gave me shots of morphine to kill the pain, otherwise I could not walk, but tomorrow my mother will bring herbal medicine from the jungle."

"I'm sorry you're not well," I say. I feel too good to dislike anyone right now, even Pepe. I'm just glad he never came to the jungle.

Months after my trip, the same American scientist who would accuse him of poaching would also accuse him of robbing and assaulting female tourists in the jungle. He provided names and phone numbers.

I brace myself to ask him for the money he still owes me.

"Ah yes, the money," he says. He glances at his watch. "I have no cash, and the bank is closed now, but we will take care of it later. Do you have a hotel? I know a very good hotel, not expensive, with air conditioning. I can reserve a room for you."

How easily he's changed the subject. It's clear I'll never see my money. I had planned on returning to the little hotel where I stayed before. Until Pepe mentioned air conditioning, the idea of a shower with a ceiling and four walls seemed the height of luxury. I had forgotten about air conditioning. Exhausted, I let Pepe reserve the room.

"Luis! Take her to the Antonio," he yells downstairs.

I am startled by his shortness when he rises to say goodbye.

Luis carries my duffel to a nondescript, boxlike building. From the bright sunlight we enter a dark lobby.

"There will be lights again soon," the manager says.

Luis leads me up a long flight of stairs. The lights, what few there are, return when we reach the landing. The long, dim, dirty hallway makes me think of Times Square hotels with hookers and pimps. This hallway, however, is empty.

I suddenly feel the shock of being back in the world. It seems so strange to see Luis here. I know I will return to my little hotel, but I allow Luis to lead me to the room. I need time to get myself together.

The small room is more like a dark cell. The window looks out on an airshaft, but sure enough there is an air conditioner.

I look at Luis. We are worlds apart, standing here. The jungle that connected us is miles away, but I still see him on the river, I still see him among the trees. "You taught me so much," I say to him, as he fidgets with the dials on the air conditioner.

"There!" he says, smiling, as the sound of the cool air fills the room the way the sounds of insects filled the jungle night.

What can I say? How can I show my gratitude? Luis holds out his hand. I take it in mine, but my eyes are filled with tears.

"*Muchas gracias!*" is all I can muster.

"*De nada,*" he says, smiling, and walks softly from the room.

15

For two days I was happy in Iquitos. I was pleased with
myself. I was grateful for the time spent at Pepe's camp.
Looking at the charming jungle paintings in the Iquitos airport, I felt the Amazon had more than satisfied my childhood
dream. In the end, leaving Pepe's camp was like leaving home. I
was stronger now, more open.

I was ready to tackle whatever the Amazon might have in store
for me next. Or so I thought, until the plane door closed. I suddenly realized I was alone. There was no Luis to protect me. I had to
remind myself that I started this trip without Luis. I was fine before
I met him. But when I arrived here, I was armed with the defenses
I brought from New York. At Pepe's camp, I let down my guard. I

lived more fully in the moment. Now I am more in touch with what I feel. Perhaps that's why I'm more afraid.

I felt safe when I landed at this airport with my guide Santiago and our little group on my first trip in the Amazon. But the airport looks different to me now. I had been warned about pickpockets and thieves, but I hadn't expected the atmosphere to be so tense. I need my defenses here, but I feel as though I've forgotten how to summon them.

I move quickly toward the exit. The dark faces and hands of taxi drivers pressed against the glass exit doors look like those of caged animals dying to escape, but the drivers are on the outside, under the night sky. I'm glad a guard is there to prevent them from entering.

Clutching my duffels, I brace myself as the guard lets me out. The crowd of drivers presses round me like a vise. Frightened, I allow the first man yelling, "Taxi!" to grab my arm. He pulls me through the crowd to his battered cab. I feel relieved until he slams the door with me inside. Then I see the driver's wild burning eyes. I am too afraid to jump out.

"How much to Hotel Delfines in Puerto Callao?" I ask him in Spanish, in my gruffest voice to hide my fear.

"Fifty *inti*," he replies, as he steps on the gas, speeding off like a madman into the night.

I wonder why the ride is so cheap as I stare out at the blackness unrelieved by a single light. I feel his eyes on me in the rear-view mirror.

"You came from Lima?" he shouts, over the rattling of the cab.

"No, Iquitos," I shout back. I'm so nervous I can barely understand his Spanish.

"Where is your home?" he asks.

"What?" I say. The cab sounds ready to fly apart.

"Where is your home?" he asks again, none too pleased to repeat himself.

"New York," I yell.

"Sit up front so we can talk," he says.

Too afraid to say no, I climb over the seat, and sit by the door. Why are there no lights on this road? I wonder, looking in vain for some way to escape.

"Where is your husband?" he asks me.

Up close, his eyes are more frightening. They seem to bore through my skull like lethal beams.

"He's in Lima," I lie. "He's coming to Yarinacocha tomorrow."

"Why does he allow you to travel alone?" he asks.

"He had to work," I say, but the driver eyes me suspiciously.

"You have a reservation at Hotel Delfines?" he asks.

"No," I foolishly reply. I feel like hitting myself for such stupidity, but the driver, who is roughly tapping my arm to emphasize his words, seems to be doing that for me.

Where will this ride end? I wonder. He could be driving me anywhere. Who would find me if something happened? Who would know where to look? I'm not sure my mother knows where the Amazon is. When I told her where I was going, she said, Have a nice trip, dear.

The brakes screech as he comes to a sudden stop.

"Where are we?" I ask, looking out at the blackness.

Ignoring my question, he holds out his hand. His eyes look like fiery coals. "Give me two hundred-fifty *inti*," he says.

My hands shaking, I pay him the money without discussion, and bolt from the cab with my bags.

The cab speeds away instantly. Any place else I would consider myself lucky, but here the world feels like a darkened movie house just before they run the film. What film will play on this screen? I wonder. The blackness gives way to an assortment of grays as my eyes grow accustomed to the darkness. A gray hulk of a building appears on top of a hill. Crumbling earth gives way to mud as I stumble to the top and find a narrow concrete path. I circle the building, but I can't find the entrance. I peek through the slats of a shuttered window. A man stands inside a lighted room. I bang on the shutter. The man motions me around to the side, where he opens a door.

"Is this Hotel Delfines?" I ask.

"Yes," says the elderly man in a hoarse voice, looking at me warily. His face has the texture of sandpaper.

"You must be Antonio," I say in Spanish, feeling almost faint with relief. "I'm a friend of Kenneth's in New York." I hand him the letter I brought.

The husky, white-haired man leads me inside a small, shabby room where a color TV plays at full volume. I think this is his living room and office. He shows me to a chair and takes a seat behind his desk.

"How is Kenneth?" Antonio asks.

Kenneth gave me precise instructions about what to tell his friends. "He hasn't come to Yarinacocha this year because he has problems buying his house."

"Did he get married?" Antonio asks.

"No, he's not married, but he's engaged," Kenneth told me to say.

Antonio grunts in approval.

He shows me to a room around the side of the house, and gives me directions to Wilfredo's restaurant before he leaves me. The bare room has a large fan and a small refrigerator stocked with Pepsi and Inca Cola. Fading newspaper pinups are tacked on the wall.

Outside, in the dark, I feel disoriented, even with a flashlight. Is there really a town here? Can this be Puerto Callao, the main village on Lake Yarinacocha?

Walking down the hill, I find a rutted path pocked with holes. My flashlight beam spotlights a few ghostly shacks in the distance.

Past the shacks, the faint sound of music grows steadily louder until I turn into a wide, dusty street ablaze with fluorescent light. The local *chicha* music assaults my ears. The bars on both sides of the street vibrate with the sound. After the stillness and darkness, this island of life seems dreamlike as I watch a drunken man, wearing only loose trousers, stagger down the street between the bars.

I find Wilfredo's restaurant easily. Kenneth said this was the only restaurant in town that washes dishes with soap.

Wilfredo, small and rotund with pomaded hair, also asks me if Kenneth is married. When I say Kenneth is engaged, he smiles slyly. "You are the fiancée?" he asks.

"No, no, I am only Kenneth's friend," I reply.

Kenneth told me his friends in Puerto Callao can't understand why a man his age isn't married. He said they probably think something is wrong with him. What will they think of me?

A slim and attractive fair-haired woman in her thirties suddenly appears like an apparition on the porch. Margrit, the Swiss wife of Kenneth's Peruvian friend, Vicente, joins me at my table.

I am disappointed that she doesn't speak English, but I am glad to have her company. Like the others she is concerned with Kenneth's marital status. When I tell her he is engaged, Margrit says, "Finally! Is she the one from California?"

Kenneth has lots of girlfriends. He didn't give me details about his imaginary fiancée, so I tell her I don't know.

"How many years have you lived here?" I ask her in Spanish.

"Eight. I love the jungle. Puerto Callao is a very peaceful place," she says, as *chicha* music blasts from the bars along the street.

A few days before my trip, power lines in Pucallpa and Yarinacocha were cut by terrorists in the mountains. There was no electricity, no communication. I considered postponing my trip even though Kenneth said that power lines were relatively new here and people would hardly miss them. The power was restored, however, before I left, so I gave no further thought to the terrorists, though Tingo María, the drug trade capital in Peru and a terrorist stronghold, is only a day's drive from Pucallpa.

I think Margrit's grasp of reality is rather tenuous, though sitting here beside her, I suppose one could say the same for me. I'm beginning to wonder what sparked my fantasies here on my first trip six month ago. Perhaps the sense of life I felt then had nothing to do with the town.

Puerto Callao was my first glimpse of the Amazon as we drove from the airport through the streets to the harbor. From the lake, on our way to the tourist lodge, metal roofs shimmered in the dying light. The air was electrified. The sky exploded like fireworks in a dazzling finale of color. The lake shone like a metallic mirror, glinting with hints of precious ores. A crowd gathered on the high bank. Pounding *chicha* rhythms celebrated nature's grand display while laughter and shouts rang out in the sultry air. Is that town here? Is this cacaphony the sound I heard then?

I say goodnight to Margrit and promise to visit her tomorrow. Wilfredo shows me the way back. "Puerto Callao is very peaceful," he says, echoing Margrit. Am I the only one who hears the noise?

Hotel Delfines, perched on a mound of dirt, looms like a dark ruin in the night. The music gives way to droning cicadas and huge croaking frogs which leap by my legs on the concrete path around the building. I fumble with the faulty lock on my door as lizards crawl along the wall and wasps linger nearby.

Switching on the dim bulb overhead throws about a dozen giant *cucarachas* on the wall above my bed into great confusion. They scramble for hiding places. I feel a wave of disgust. I grab the repellent at the bottom of my duffel. Kenneth thought I was crazy to bring an insect spray to the jungle, but I brought this spray precisely for nightmares like this.

The powerful fumes threaten me as much as the bugs. A poison mist hangs in the air as each cockroach, about three inches long, drops to the floor with a thump. I feel thoroughly revolted. No other insects arouse my revulsion like cockroaches. At Pepe's camp, I chased them from my food, but I didn't see them in the hut where I slept. Here, I don't even have a mosquito net! I feel as though a hundred creatures are crawling on my skin.

I spray two more cockroaches emerging from the darkness. I wish I could air the room, but if I open the door who knows what might fly or crawl inside.

I suddenly remember I haven't locked the door. When I turn the lock, the rusted knob falls into my hand.

16

In early morning, my first view of Puerto Callao outside the hotel doesn't improve my mood. Under the jumble of oddly angled metal roofs gleaming in the harsh light, one-story buildings, sheds, and stalls look like patchwork quilts of rusted metal and weathered wood. The air feels as hot as a furnace. The smells of jungle rot, fuel, excrement and urine make my head reel. Down the hill vultures perch on piles of garbage. Telephone poles lean at crazy angles. Boys on unmuffled motorcycles zoom by, raising clouds of dust. A broken-down bus from Pucallpa discharges bedraggled passengers. Headed toward the port a block away, boys ride in the back of open trucks.

"Why didn't you come to me last night?" Antonio says, hugging me like a daughter when I tell him about the cockroaches.

He assures me my new room will be free of bugs. I'd like to believe him.

I can't wait to buy bottled water at the bodega on the corner of the wide dirt street where I walked last night. But the bodega doesn't sell bottled water. The woman behind the counter tells me bottled water isn't sold in Puerto Callao. They do sell doughy rolls in plastic bags, however, that feel like sponges.

Walking toward the port, I pass a little market with tiny stalls selling limp cotton dresses. Rickety tables display buttons and safety pins, combs and spools of thread, shoes and T-shirts.

The lake looks less than inviting. Children bathe and women wash clothes near sewage and oil spills from the boats. At the far end of the port stand two fishing boats. In the center, several large, covered boats called *pegue-pegues* because of the sound of the outboard motors, ferry locals to nearby villages. At the other end, more *pegue-pegues* await tourists. Off to the side by the lake, the electric plant looks out of place.

It wasn't until the early 1930s that settlers began to migrate here. In the beginning, they lived off the land and the lake, farming, hunting, and fishing. When a road opened, connecting Yarinacocha with Pucallpa in the late thirties, trade began. Cash eventually replaced the barter system. In the mid-forties, the village of Puerto Callao was founded.

Today, despite small factories, farming and fishing still provide the main income. But the influx of people living around the lake has driven away many of the fish. Overfishing has further depleted the supply. Giant *paiche* have disappeared. Manatees, turtles, and caimans have vanished. Commercial fishermen go fifty or more kilometers away to find the fish sold in the market. Subsistence living is declining in small mestizo and native settlements. To help farmers, the government, which set up cooperatives, buys the rice crop, but payments are erratic.

It's no wonder some mestizos and Shipibo go to work for dollars in the fields around Tingo María, in the Upper Huallaga Valley, where perhaps half of the world's coca leaves are grown. Both the Shining Path and the Tupac Amaru are funded by the cocaine trade and have gained a stronghold there. This stronghold is stimulated in part by the U.S. drug war, which, by wiping out coca plants, has deprived otherwise poverty-stricken settlers of their livelihood. Meanwhile, more and more settlers plant coca, which they sell at a relatively high profit to cocaine processors.

From the dried leaves, coca paste is extracted and then flown by middlemen to labs in Colombia for processing: by some accounts, Peru's drug trade provides a third of its export income.

After working in the coca fields, some of those who return to Yarinacocha are drug dealers or addicts. Incidents of violence are often related to drugs.

The bus route along the Trans-Andean Highway from Tinga Maria to Pucallpa is used by smugglers. Several times women were caught carrying dead babies on board, the corpses stuffed with bags of coca paste.

Puerto Callao is an unlikely tourist town, but residents of Pucallpa like to relax here on weekends. Today, however, is a weekday, and several idle boys with *pegue-pegues* see dollar signs when they look at me.

"I give you special price to Shipibo village," one says.

"I take you anywhere you want to go very cheap," says another.

While I breakfast on the waterfront, a tall young mestizo joins me. His broad smile says he wants to sell me something too.

"I show you villages where Indians still paint their faces," he says. "I am very good guide. I have very good boat. I take you on the river for a week at very good price."

"Thank you, but I just arrived. I'm not ready for a river trip," I tell him, as I eat my half-cooked egg.

I wish I could see the town and the lake the way I saw them last time. I want to feel open here, but everything I see repels me. Was coming back a mistake? The words of the poet Elizabeth Bishop keep running through my mind. "...they have changed; you have changed; even the weather may have changed."

The Ucayali River is always changing. In fact, maps can't keep up with it. Oxbow lakes like Yarinacocha were formed when the Ucayali changed its course.

Looking out at the lake, I wonder if I should change my course. Maybe I'll feel better staying at the tourist lodge again. I see now that Pepe's camp was easy. I didn't have to make decisions. I was led by the hand like a child.

The lodge doesn't have a phone so I hire one of the overly eager boys with a *pegue-pegue* to take me there to reserve a room for tomorrow. The lodge is nearby on the lake.

As I board, I hear someone say, "Good morning!" I turn and see Wilfredo, the restaurant owner, in swimming trunks, bathing beside the boat. He is covered with soapsuds. He dries his hand and gives me a hearty handshake. "How are you this morning?" he says, smiling.

This simple human gesture makes me forget my revulsion for the town. I am moved. To this man, the world is perfectly fine this morning. From the boat, I watch him duck underwater, rise and throw back his head, shaking water from his face like the stray dogs bathing nearby.

Even from a distance Puerto Callao looks like an open wound. Around the crescent-shaped lake, which changes size with the floods but appears now about seven miles long, the valuable trees like cedar and mahogany were taken long ago by loggers. In the last decades, trees have been cleared for settlements and small family gardens of yucca and bananas. The forest I see now is secondary growth.

The northern end of the lake is the site of the oldest known village in the upper Amazon. A tribe of less than a thousand people known as the Tutiscainyo lived there for one or two centuries between 2000 and 1600 BC. At that time another lake or channel of the Ucayali flowed by the village. The Tutiscainyo were skilled potters. At night they probably filled their closed huts with smoke to ward off mosquitoes.

The mosquitoes haven't changed, but everything else has. Even the *Yarina* palms, which gave the lake its name, seem to have vanished. I can't help missing the powerful presence of the jungle along the Yarapa River. Here, the forest looks bland.

The most arresting sight seems to be the huge circular tourist lodge of wood and thatch, rising like an indigenous palace between the trees. It looks large enough to house an entire tribe, but the owner is an American who built the lodge ten years ago with his wife.

I see the wife on board a *pegue-pegue* with some tourists heading out on the water. I've never yelled across a lake before to reserve a room, but this seems to be the easiest solution. The wife yells back, says she'll have a room ready tomorrow morning.

I watch two hydroplanes land behind the trees obscuring the compound of the Summer Institute of Linguistics, a Protestant missionary group who made Yarinacocha their base in the mid-forties. Since then, they have translated the Bible into native languages all over the Amazon. In Peru alone, there are over fifty indigenous Indian groups. Whatever one may think of the *linguisticos,* as they are called here, they did teach the Indians to read and write, preparing them for contact with the outside world. All the tribes have been more or less contaminated by the West. It's too late to wish the Indians had been left alone. I only hope their cultures will not be completely lost.

Back in town, I find Antonio behind his hotel, weeding a patch of earth he calls his garden. He proudly shows me some violet flowers shriveling near a muddy ditch where vultures perch and flies and mosquitoes make their home. The garden is his passion, so I try to share his enthusiasm.

Sweat drips down my face and my hair feels as wet as it was in the shower, as I follow Antonio's directions to the house of Kenneth's friend, Margrit, the Swiss woman I met at Wilfredo's restaurant.

The simple wooden structure, painted brown, stands out among the shanties.

Margrit's husband, Vicente, a builder in Pucallpa, answers the door in a towel. He's one of the handsomest men I've ever seen.

"I'm late for work," he says in apology, leading me into a sparsely furnished but tasteful room, cooled by a fan. I marvel that the little room is spotless.

Looking like a suburban hostess in a fresh white jumpsuit, Margrit carries a tray with lemonade from the kitchen.

As we settle into canvas chairs, Margrit fusses over her three-year-old son whose body is covered by a rash.

After Vicente leaves, Margrit says, "Vicente's friends in Lima always tell him how much money he could be making there. They don't understand that we're not interested in money. We just want a simple life. In Switzerland, no one understands that either. My mother is horrified that I live in the jungle. She's never met Vicente or our son."

I think Margrit should be happy her mother has never seen this place, but I keep my opinion to myself. Instead, I ask, "How did you happen to come here?"

"My first husband was Swiss," she says. "He came here to work for an oil company. When I met Vicente, my marriage was breaking up. Vicente's marriage was ending too. He has a daughter who also lives with us. She's at school now in Pucallpa."

"You don't miss Europe?" I ask her.

"Oh no, everything I want is here. I have my children, my husband, my home. I'm happy being a housewife."

"I wish I could see what you like about this town," I say, deciding to be honest.

Margrit laughs. "It just takes time," she says, as she sweeps bits of dust from the table into her hand.

Margrit is a mystery to me. I can understand the romance of living in virgin jungle, but why would anyone choose to live here?

On the waterfront, I watch while the town assembles for the evening market. Fishermen climb the steep banks with sacks on their backs. The noise from the outboard motors competes with the sellers hawking fish and the throbbing music from the bars. Barefoot women crouch beside piles of squirming fish. Mangy dogs sniff mounds of corn, papayas, avocados, bananas. Men and boys on motorcycles and bicycles stream into the market while others lug wheelbarrows with fresh fruit. Trucks pull up by the harbor, and latecomers unload baskets and sacks from canoes. Venders sell cigarettes, one at a time, and Chiclets on trays. Women cook meat on skewers.

In the sky, long strips of iridescent pink turn to violet and violet-blue before fading. The first stars shine. Set free from the heat, the town seems to breathe and expand as though a great weight has been lifted.

I feel a weight lifting from my shoulders as well. For the first time I feel as though I'm really here. I am seeing Puerto Callao without the weight of my expectations. This is the Puerto Callao I remember. I didn't make it up. It wasn't a dream, unless I am dreaming now. The smells have vanished. There is a sweetness in the air. The faces that looked so dull all day have suddenly come to life. Maybe Margrit was right. Maybe I just need time here.

17

Last night I didn't find cockroaches in my room, but I did find a dead tarantula. Despite the tarantula, I thought I would see Puerto Callao with different eyes this morning after feeling the magic that happens here at sunset. But the town looks as repulsive in daylight as it looked before.

I should be glad I can escape to the tourist lodge, but I have mixed feelings about staying there again. At the lodge I'll feel safe. But I feel as though I'm running away. I'm giving up. Isn't the real challenge staying in Puerto Callao and working through my revulsion? Isn't the real challenge to find some redeeming value in this town? It is, but I'm in no mood for more challenges. Right now I need to escape, to feel safe.

"Weren't you here before?" asks George, the owner of the jungle lodge, as he carries my duffels from the dock. The tall, mustachioed man about fifty has a face that reminds me of a walrus.

I'm surprised that I even look familiar to him. He didn't show much interest in his guests last time I was here. I was glad his wife took charge of our visit. His slightly disdainful air put me off, though he and my guide Santiago were buddies. This morning, however, he seems pleasant enough.

"Kurt and Greta are going out in the *pegue-pegue* to spot some birds," George says, speaking about the lone couple having breakfast in the restaurant. "If you join them, you can share expenses."

It seems too late in the morning to spot birds, but I have nothing else to do. The young couple, in stylish safari clothes, look at me warily. I decide to join them anyway.

"Are you really traveling alone?" Greta asks, her eyes wide behind her glasses, as the boat heads out into the lake.

"Yes," I reply.

"Aren't you afraid?" she asks.

"Sometimes. I've had a few bad moments," I reply.

"We saw you yesterday on the boat. Did you stay in that awful town?" she asks.

"Yes."

She and Kurt, who brushes an insect from his neatly trimmed beard, are looking at me as though I belong to an alien species. I felt more comfortable in Puerto Callao than I feel with them.

A labyrinth of canals cuts through the forest beyond the lake. The forest is thick and green. It looks too pretty. Lone Shipibo huts with little steps cut in the high banks occasionally interrupt the greenness. Besides the inevitable kingfishers and the mosquitoes swirling around our heads, nothing moves in the heat. The boat feels too large and unwieldy for the narrow canals littered with fallen trees. I'm not surprised when it snags on a submerged log.

Cursing, the boatboy, in waist-high water, rocks the boat to loosen it. To lighten the load, I climb out on a log. I feel like an old pro on the river.

Hour after hour passes. The boat moves slowly. We see no birds. I am bored and drowsy. I doze off. When the boat snags on a tree with branches rising from the center of the canal, I am glad there is finally an event to keep me awake. The boatboy must have dozed, too, otherwise he would have seen this obstacle.

Angrily, as though this mishap was our fault, the boy gestures for one of us to leave. Kurt volunteers when he sees that I have no intention of moving.

"Give me the camera!" Greta shouts, as Kurt steps out on a log.

"The camera will be fine," he shouts back.

"I won't let you ruin that camera!" she screams.

Kurt wavers on the log, lurching forward as he hands it to her, but he manages to regain his balance.

"See what you almost made me do!" he yells, his face red while the boatboy, still cursing, tries to push the boat.

Naked Shipibo children, watching from the top of the bank, double over in fits of laughter. I wish I felt so amused.

While the boatboy struggles, Shipibo fishermen in slender dugouts paddle past us without a glance in our direction. Their canoes, a quarter the size of the *pegue-pegue*, weave through the canal with ease. The canals are their trails through the forest.

The boatboy, a mestizo, is reluctant to demean himself by asking for their help. Mestizos consider the Shipibo "uncivilized," and look down on them. But the Shipibo — at least the ones who remain in their villages — have no desire for the mestizo way of life. The Indians see no reason to help us.

In desperation, the boatboy finally hails one of their canoes. He offers a wiry, broad-shouldered fisherman a couple of coins to dislodge the boat, which he does, singlehandedly, in only a few minutes.

We continue slowly through the narrow canals. Our mishaps have dispelled the tension between me and the Germans. I'm not surprised when Kurt tells me he's a banker. Greta is an economics student.

"I won't be sorry to leave the jungle," Greta says. "Four weeks in Peru is enough for me."

"Where do you go from here?" I ask.

"Margarita Island in Venezuela," she says, sighing. "I can't wait to lie on a clean white beach and stay in a modern hotel."

The boatboy points to an army of dark clouds rolling our way. "We better go back," he says.

A few minutes later, the sky darkens, and a torrent of rain washes over the boat. I want to close my eyes and pretend this day never happened, but the lashing wind and rain won't let me.

The boatboy picks up two mestizo women waving wildly on the bank. They giggle. Their soaked dresses cling to their skin. I think the women inspire the boy, who guides the boat with greater skill through the choppy water than he did when the water was calm.

To console myself, I try to imagine Amazon river trips far worse than this one. In Brazil in 1850, the great naturalist Alfred Russell Wallace and his crew of paddlers fought against a current so fast the crew was powerless against it. On this dangerous river, the crew carried the canoe and provisions over slippery rocks, around wild and furious waterfalls.

As the hours slip away, I am too wet and cold, however, to find consolation from others' trips.

Finally, we reach the turbulent lake, a small sea of white caps. We pull up to the lodge after dark. We never did spot any birds.

The storm rages while I dine in the dimly lit restaurant under a thatched dome nearly sixty feet high. This is not a place to be alone. Months ago I was sitting here with my guide Santiago. I had a crush on him. I wonder where he is now. I wonder if I would feel differently here if he suddenly came through that door.

But I am not the same person I was on my first trip. I can't see the lake, the lodge, or the town with the innocent eyes I had then when the jungle was new to me and I had nothing to compare it to except my childhood dream.

My thoughts are interrupted when the screen door flies open and two disheveled figures in wet ponchos enter the restaurant.

George, the lodge owner, told me an English woman he had met in town was looking for someone to share the cost of a river trip. When he told her about me, she said she'd come to the lodge tonight.

Lucy can't be more than twenty. With one long earring and a lavender streak in her blond crewcut, the small plump English girl seems an unlikely companion for a river trip. She is accompanied by a girl named Soledad, a mestizo about eighteen, who says she is George's secretary.

They settle into the awkward handmade chairs around my table, which has a fish carved in the sloping top.

"What weather! I really need a beer," Lucy says, turning to George who has joined us. He goes off to get a round of drinks. I'm surprised to see him so docile. He has boys who usually do this sort of thing.

I wonder how I missed seeing Lucy in town. "How long have you been here?" I ask her.

"I arrived last night from Lima," she says. "I thought I'd see the jungle before I go to Cuzco, but I'll be in Peru for nine months, so I'm sure I'll have time to see everything.

"I just hope the hotels in Cuzco will be better than the dump I found on the waterfront. I'll have to get drunk to sleep on that bed again! I swear there must be rocks inside that mattress. And I woke up this morning with bites all over me even though I slept under my portable mosquito net. I saw a big bug on the wall, but do you think there could be bedbugs?"

"There's no shortage of bugs in Puerto Callao," I reply.

Changing the subject, Lucy says, "I met a chap on the dock this morning who said he'll give us a really good deal on a river trip."

I laugh. "After the day I spent on the river, I can't face another trip right now. Maybe I'll feel differently tomorrow," I add, seeing her disappointment.

"There's nothing else to do here as far as I can see," Lucy says. "I saw the whole town in twenty minutes." She pauses. "I guess I'll go alone then."

"If I were you, I'd try to meet several guides before I choose one," I say to her.

"That's probably a good idea," she replies.

"I have some very good guides," George says, returning with the drinks. "I can introduce you to them tomorrow."

Maybe I was wrong about George. He seems helpful.

Soledad hasn't said a word, but she bothers me. Her little smile seems to hide some secret. With her sharp eyes, she follows every word, every gesture. She watches Lucy most of all.

"I love your earring," she says to Lucy. "I wanted to wear earrings so much one night I took a needle and pierced my ears myself."

"Didn't that hurt?" I ask, looking at the five or six tiny gold dots in each of her ears.

"No, it wasn't bad. I'm tough," she says, grinning.

When Soledad leaves, Lucy says, "I wish I could afford to stay here. What beautiful tables and chairs!"

"The furniture was made by a local sculptor," George says. "He agreed to do all this work for only $1000. It took him ten months. When he finished, he wanted more money, but I said, "'No. You agreed to that price.'"

George looks pleased with himself. It disgusts me to hear about artists being exploited, but in this case I don't feel that bad. Kenneth told me about this artist, who sometimes claims to be a shaman and gives ayahuasca — which can be dangerous — to tourists who want to try the hallucinogenic drug.

To change the subject, I ask George if Santiago has brought any tours to the lodge lately, but George's attention is focused on Lucy. When he says no, I wonder if he heard what I said.

As George moves closer to Lucy, Lucy inches away. I take this as my cue to leave, but as I walk along the covered ramp to my bungalow, I wonder if I am wrong to leave Lucy alone with George.

18

Blobs of mud splatter the windows of George's Volkswagen, so I can barely see the road to Pucallpa. When the mud gives way to paved streets in the center of the city, I'm surprised the trip from the lodge took less than thirty minutes.

Pucallpa isn't a place of beauty, but it is the capital of the newly formed department of Ucayali and the boom town of the Peruvian Amazon, with more than 90,000 people.

Pucallpa doesn't feel like a boom town. It barely feels like a city. Asphalt streets cover roughly one square mile. Sewers and electricity are confined to the center.

I follow George with Kurt, the German banker, along the dusty sidewalks lined with sleazy hotels, juice bars, and stores selling bolts of cheap cloth, ropes and twine, shotgun shells, and huge blades for saws that cut timber. I see glass-walled banks, a movie theater, and a couple of hotels that look better than the rest, but the atmosphere reminds me of Wild West frontier towns I've seen in the movies. With all the thieves and drug smugglers here, I wouldn't be surprised to see a shoot-out.

The smells are even worse than those in Puerto Callao, but Puerto Callao doesn't have an oil refinery, a paper mill, plywood factories, and sawmills surrounding it. With the support of multi-national companies supplying technology and expertise, the government is eager to exploit the timber and oil in the jungle to help pay off its huge foreign debt.

When development takes place within Indian territories, the Indians, ironically, must prove they are entitled to land they have lived on for thousands of years.

At the turn of the century in Pucallpa when the Cashibo Indians were displaced by a rubber tappers' camp, the idea of legally protecting their lands was unknown. Rubber was prized here long before timber and oil. When the boom ended, the former rubber tappers built a village of cane and thatch huts widely scattered in the jungle. Around 1920, the American adventurer, Harry L. Forster, saw the village a few months after it had been totally destroyed by floods that killed their cattle and ruined their crops. The village had been rebuilt above a high bank. Five years earlier, the Ucayali had flowed a mile away from the village. The settlers showed him the dried-out riverbed covered with forest.

Without the Trans-Andean Highway, which opened in 1930, Pucallpa might still be a village. But the mud and gravel road — closed after rains and so narrow traffic could move only in one direction on a given day — paved the way for Pucallpa's expansion. It wasn't until the seventies, however, that the road was completely surfaced. Now that it's used year-round, heavy machinery is transported more easily to develop the interior, and goods flow faster from the jungle.

During World War II, rubber once again played a part in Pucallpa's destiny. The United States was cut off from rubber in the Far East, so it turned to Pucallpa to meet its supply. By 1940 Pucallpa had 5,000 residents. But the need for rubber was short-lived. After the war, a small oil strike and the building of a refinery providing cheap fuel on the Ucayali kept the town going.

The large indoor market, reeking of fish, is going strong when we arrive. A stall with dried herbs and unmarked bottles of herbal medicines looks intriguing. The old woman behind the counter tries to persuade me to drink a thick black liquid that is good for digestion, she says. I tell her my digestion is fine. She pours the brew into a shot glass anyway, but I don't have the nerve to try it.

George leaves Kurt and me outside the market. Kurt hasn't stopped complaining about his wife since early this morning, but I'm glad he's here with me in Pucallpa. This town feels rough, like sandpaper scraping my skin.

We hail a taxi to the port. Past the center, the taxi drives through rutted streets lined with blackened shacks, some shaped like trape-zoids. The shacks look more like pig sties than human shelters.

The deep puddles grow nearly impassable. Beside an outdoor market on the high bank, the driver stops before a large pig, at home in the mud.

Wood planks, too far apart to be of much use, serve as walkways. My feet and legs are soon covered with slime. I feel as though I'm sloshing through deep snow.

Across from the market and a muddy pool as big as a creek, nomads live in more hovels, thrown together with boards and patched with scrap metal. This place looks filthier than Belén.

"I'm glad Greta didn't come," Kurt remarks. Earlier, he said Greta claimed to be sick this morning because she didn't want to get her shoes dirty.

Standing away from the crowded market — where the faces are less than friendly — we look down at dark greasy water with swirls of oil. A long canoe anchors itself by running onto the debris-strewn bank. Vultures almost outnumber the people, swarming around cargo boats, barges, dugouts, ferries, river boats. Clumps of bananas lie in mud.

Three men, weighed down by an eight-foot *paiche,* slowly climb the bank. Women in shapeless dresses carry babies up trembling gangplanks, which are nothing more than narrow boards.

In contrast to the port, the cafe at the Hotel Mercedes seems the height of civilization. Next to our table, three light-skinned women with carefully made-up faces and fairly fashionable clothes talk in low tones. I wonder if they've ever seen the port. The distance between the upper and lower classes in Peru is greater than the distance from the desert to the highest Andean peak. For hundreds of years, economic power has been in the hands of the white upper class.

These light-skinned women, probably wives of businessmen or local officials, are part of a small well-educated and sophisticated elite from the coast, made up of mestizos and *criollos,* Peruvian born descendants of Spaniards who identify with the aristocratic culture of Lima. Both mestizos, who make up most of Peru's population, and criollos have disdain for the jungle.

The jungle is beset by ethnic and racial conflicts that keep settlers from working together to take power from the elite. The settlers, many of highland Indian origin, consider themselves civilized, an idea advanced by missionaries. Committed to progress and the conquest of the jungle, they nevertheless distrust settlers from other Andean villages and consider jungle Indians who preserve their traditions uncivilized. They exploit the Indians in land and lumber disputes. Settlers, in turn, are exploited by middlemen who buy their crops, and by the state bureaucracy, which excels in mismanagement. While a growing number of settlers grow coca at the fringes of the jungle in order to feed their families, mestizos and criollos send their children to school in Lima and relax at the Hotel Mercedes cafe.

But even here in this gathering place of the elite, my toast is served cold.

At breakfast, Kurt is still complaining about his wife.

"I try not to take Greta on my climbing trips," he says. "I took her with me once. After the first two hours, I carried her pack. After the next two hours, I carried her."

I'm glad when Soledad, George's secretary, joins us, even though her little smile still seems to hide a smirk. I can imagine her alone in her room at the lodge, laughing at us all.

Wearing native skirts and short ruffled blouses, two barefoot Shipibo women stand in the doorway, hissing to get our attention. They peddle necklaces and bows and arrows.

When George arrives, I leave with Soledad to meet Lucy, the English girl, in Puerto Callao. I've had enough of Kurt for one morning.

In the taxi, Soledad says, smiling, "I am like part of George's family. He loves me like a daughter. He would do anything for me."

"Where is your own family?" I ask her.

"They are in my village. But I live here permanently now with George and Sarah. Isn't my English good? I taught myself English in my village."

"Yes, your English is very good," I tell her. "Don't you ever see your family?"

"Once in a while," she says. "But I like my life better here. I like my new family. I like meeting tourists. I make many friends."

I try to imagine Soledad without that smile.

At Wilfredo's restaurant, Lucy tells me she has arranged a four-day river trip for tomorrow with a guide she met through George. "Are you sure you don't want to come?" she asks me.

I shake my head, no.

"What will you do here?" Lucy asks.

"That's a good question," I reply.

What am I doing here now, I wonder, with Lucy and Soledad who are young enough to be my daughters. I feel adrift, without a purpose, without a plan. I came here wanting to see Shipibo villages. But now the thought of seeing those villages depresses me. The unwalled huts of the Shipibo along the canals and around the lake look so melancholy. I'm afraid their villages will disappoint me as much as the town and the lodge. I'm not excited by the prospect of being cold and wet for days on end in a *pegue-pegue* along the river.

My first day here I browsed through the Shipibo co-op market. Kenneth had warned me about the co-op. He said artists never sell their best work there. The co-op is a tourist market. Hundreds of crudely fashioned and carelessly painted jars and pots were jammed on shelves from floor to ceiling. I wondered if somewhere in the jungle an assembly line of artists had produced these wares. I had found the bargain basement of Shipibo art.

In the exhibition room in back, I found some finer pieces, but the couple in the store refused to sell them. The couple was intrigued by my cheap watch with its silver band. I took it off so they could examine it more closely. "How much did it cost?" they asked me. "Where did you buy it?"

The sun breaks through the clouds for the first time today. I have to do something. I have to try. But try what? Maybe a hike near the lodge. When I suggest it, Lucy wants to hike, too.

We hire a boat to take us to the lodge. George sends one of his guides to lead us on the trail which begins by the lake. Our guide shouts to a man named Angel, painting his *pegue-pegue* by the water. Lucy says, "George told me Angel is his best guide, but I couldn't find him this morning."

Away from the port, the lake doesn't look so bad. I climb down the bank to meet Angel, a small, wiry man with a grizzled face who is working beside his teenage son, also named Angel. Grinning from ear to ear, Angel senior bows as he shakes my hand. He seems amiable, but I'm cautious. I arrange two day-trips, for which he asks me to pay in advance. I feel better handing him the money. I have a plan now.

My mood improves as the trail winds away from the water. Cultivated fruit trees give way to second-growth jungle, which is thicker underfoot than primary forest.

Lucy's enthusiasm for the forest is equalled only by her revulsion for the insects. Her "oohs," "aahs," and "ughs" get on my nerves, but at least she is lively.

Over a broad stream we cross a makeshift bridge. I think fallen trees were used as its model. The dubious framework supports logs inclined in various directions. As the bridge quivers, I hang on to a wooden rail tied with vines.

In a tall cecropia tree, a sloth hangs upside down on the end of a high branch. The creature looks like a clump of grayish-green leaves. Watching its arm move is like watching a film in slow motion.

Making a loop, we return to the lodge as the sun sets. I wait on shore while Lucy, in her underwear, takes a dip in the lake.

Emerging from the water in the darkness, she examines her arms and legs in horror. She is covered by bites. "What bit me?" she screams. "I didn't feel a thing in the water. Christ, bugs follow me everywhere! I can't even lose them when I sleep!"

"Why don't you stay at Antonio's hotel with me?" I say to Lucy. I've had enough of George and the lodge. "I can't promise you won't find bugs, but the beds are comfortable, and Antonio's a nice old man."

"No hotel could be worse than the dump where I'm staying now," Lucy says.

In the evening, at the restaurant of the Hotel Mercedes in Pucallpa, where we decided to splurge on dinner after checking into Antonio's hotel, Lucy says, "I worked in a shop all year and shared a flat with a girl in London before I came here. I couldn't stand the thought of more school! I want to be a writer, but what can you write about if you live your life in other people's books?"

"I didn't go to school either," I say to her, "and I'm not sorry." I see myself in Lucy. I feel as though I've found a younger sister.

The dining room of the Hotel Mercedes has white table cloths and waiters in uniform, but the walls need paint and the mood is one of decaying elegance. The only guests beside Lucy and myself are a large group of Americans. I wonder if they are *linguisticos* from the Summer Institute. The women's clothing looks dated, and some wear hair styles that remind me of films from the forties.

"This place is a pit!" Lucy says, laughing. She looks over at the Americans and shakes her head. "If this is the height of nightlife in Pucallpa, you won't find me here long!"

"I thought it would be so different!" I say, laughing. My laughter bursts forth in waves that keep me breathless. Lucy's laughter echoes my own. She doubles over, her body shaking. How absurd, sitting here in this ramshackle town, mere specks in this vast jungle.

19

Breakfast with my guide Angel and his son on board the *pegue-pegue* is not a culinary delight. I don't mind the finger bananas and the cellophane package of saltine crackers. But I decline the Pepsi as we pull up to the bank of San Francisco, the nearest Shipibo village, on the northern end of Yarinacocha. I follow Angel up the steep slope and along a narrow trail. He walks so fast I can barely keep up. He laughs when I slip and nearly fall. I have a feeling Angel's company will not enhance this day-trip.

As we enter the village, rows of schoolchildren, in green and white uniforms, are singing the national anthem while the Peruvian flag is raised. A row of solemn men, each wearing a *cushma*, the traditional Shipibo poncho, look on from the shade of a hut. "Is this a graduation ceremony?" I ask Angel, but he doesn't know.

I am struck by the order and cleanliness of the village — the long, straight rows of huts, cooking sheds, pottery sheds, chicken coops; but it reminds me of a military post. The straight rows resemble the pattern of American streets. I suspect the Summer Institute has played a part in this arrangement. The missionaries began their work here in the forties.

Shadows as sharp as razors cut the wide, well-swept paths between the huts where people lie in hammocks. They are so still they look like wax figures.

The village I saw last time seemed so different. A group of girls giggled when we approached. Here, they act as though we don't exist. No one glances in our direction. But the hostility in the air is thick enough to touch.

The Shipibo mind their own business. I think they wish we would do the same. We're intruders, voyeurs. But I'm too fascinated to leave. The women look fierce, almost leonine, reclining in their beautifully embroidered native skirts. I see great pride in their sullen faces, which seem hammered out of tawny metal. I haven't a clue as to who they are. They see the world from a perspective that I will never see. Only their hostility is recognizable to me.

The women are more imposing than the men. I sense their power. As the respected heads of family compounds — a compound is composed of several huts — they have more power than women in other tribes. They keep the culture alive. They are the artists. The villages are matrilocal. When a man marries, he moves into his wife's compound and lives among her relatives. Women can even choose when to have children. They use a contraceptive called *piripiri*.

The female puberty rites used to be the most important Shipibo event. Hundreds were invited to celebrate. Singing, dancing, and drinking could last several days or several weeks. During the feast, clitorectomies were performed on pubescent girls to prepare them for marriage. Missionaries and the Peruvian government have outlawed this practice. In San Francisco, the last initiation rites took place in the fifties.

Women may play decisive roles in everyday life, but they can never be shamans. The freedom they have is partly due to the fact that the men traditionally devote much time to spiritual matters. So the women do as they please while the men gather for shamanic sessions.

Despite ritual activities men have abandoned their *cushmas* for Western clothes and seem less bound by tradition. Some of them work outside the village for cash, clearing fields or lumbering, although farming and fishing are still their main occupations.

Their huts are unwalled to allow for breezes, but the Shipibo are discrete when it comes to glancing at their neighbors. Among themselves they are polite, modest, and reserved. Only at fiestas and manioc beer bashes do they discard their restraint and vent their aggression, both physically and verbally.

Although tribal warfare is a thing of the past, animosities between tribes continue. The Shipibo are river travelers and skilled fishermen who keep away from the forests. For as long as anyone can recall, they have considered the inland tribes barbaric. It was the custom for their war parties to kill the men and take the women and children as slaves. They believed they were saving their hostages from cannibalism.

Shipibo attacks were not limited to those made on enemy tribes. The Catholic missions, which opened in the early seventeenth century, were also besieged. Missionaries were not the only outsiders to incense the Shipibo.

Rubber companies displaced many tribes in the early part of this century and took advantage of the animosities between them.

Conibo Indians are enemies of the Campa. In payment for rifles the rubber companies *gave* the Conibo, they demanded Campa slaves to tap their rubber. The companies also gave rifles to the Campa, and demanded Conibo slaves in return.

Despite the oppressive conditions of the rubber camps and the persistence of Franciscan missionaries, who saw their chance to "save the souls" of enslaved Indians, the Shipibo managed to keep their independent spirit. In fact, the tribe has grown since the rubber boom. About 20,000 live along the fertile Ucayali river banks. Experts attribute their growth to the pride they have in themselves as a group.

But their identity as Indians is continually attacked by settlers. The Shipibo have always chosen selectively from Western culture. They value literacy and Western medicine. But the young value transister radios more than tribal stories and songs. Most young men try to find work in Pucallpa. When they do, they return to their villages only for visits.

"On Sunday nobody works, everybody drinks," Angel says.

The Shipibo don't look as though they've been drinking. But drunk or sober, they seem too intimidating to approach. I ask Angel to find Kenneth's river guide, Enrique, who lives here with his family. I have a letter for him from New York.

Angel stops at several huts. At the first two, they don't know Enrique. At the next, a woman points us in the right direction.

The Shipibo eye my camera suspiciously. They dislike being photographed, and feel ripped off by foreigners who've sold their pictures to magazines and paid them nothing. But they do allow themselves to be photographed by those who buy their pottery and textiles.

We find Enrique and his wife at the other end of the village. When I introduce myself as Kenneth's friend, Enrique and his wife smile. I'm amazed to see so much gleaming metal in their mouths.

I've never seen so much dental work before.

"You've come all this way to bring me this letter?" Enrique asks.

"Yes," I reply, thinking this is what he wants to hear.

Instead, Enrique looks shocked, then amused. I feel like a fool as they burst out laughing. I allow Angel to pull me away without any resistance.

I recover from my humiliation on the porch of a walled hut at the edge of the village. As a consolation, Angel gives me some finger bananas. A few feet from us stands a woman, holding a baby in her arms. I can't tell if Angel knows this woman or whether he's just appropriated her porch. She acts as though we are invisible, though I can hardly keep from staring at her.

She is delicate and small-boned. Above her embroidered skirt, she wears the short ruffled blouse introduced by the missionaries. Her long straight hair is dyed blue-black. A black dye is used on the baby's head as well to ward off evil spirits.

The woman seems made of stone as the baby's urine leaks through her hands, and streams down her legs and bare feet onto the palm bark floor.

Walking back through the village, I see three delicately painted bowls in one of the huts. I ask the artist how much she wants for one of them. The girl looks at me with a bored and haughty expression. "One hundred *inti*," she says, in Spanish. I love to bargain, and bargaining is the custom here. I am glad to have one more chance to make contact with the Shipibo.

The girl agrees to eighty *inti*, which is less than three dollars, but when she sees my hundred inti note — I have no change — she looks at me defiantly. "I want one hundred!" she says, grabbing the bill, and waving it in her hand.

"You agreed to eighty," I remind her.

I don't care about twenty *inti*. In fact, I feel a bit guilty bargaining her down. But if I pay what she asks, I'm afraid she'll think I'm a fool. What matters to me in this game is playing by the rules.

The girl shakes her head vehermently. "One hundred! No less!" she says, her eyes filled with hatred.

Her hostility is so unsettling I don't want the bowl at any price. "Give me back my money," I say to her.

She flings the bill in my face, and stomps off to her hammock.

I have no qualms about leaving San Francisco. I think too many people have intruded on this village: besides missionaries, anthropologists, and tourists, archaeologists came here in the fifties and discovered pottery from three ancient cultures. Recently, a television crew filmed San Francisco for a documentary on South America.

Not far from San Francisco is the small dusty village of Santa Clara. This is the settlement I saw six months ago. The thatched roofs around the hilly soccer field look as though a hundred storms have lashed their woven fronds. Angel approaches the first sagging hut where the well-worn roof nearly reaches the floor. "Do you have pots?" he asks a chubby girl who peeks out of the darkness from a hammock where she lies with her husband who is drunk. He raises his bottle to us in greeting.

"Yes," she says, smiling.

From a roof beam, she brings me three small pots, but they look like pots from the co-op market. When I smile, and shake my head, no, she lowers the price. When at last she understands that I don't want them, she looks disappointed.

I pass out gifts to the giggling children gathered around me while Angel yells through the village, "The gringa is looking for pots!" I wish he could be more subtle.

The women smile, and shake their heads, no.

"This village is backward," Angel says, scornfully, as a teenage girl walks past, wearing a bra and a native skirt.

"These women are friendlier than the ones in San Franciso," I say to him.

The mother of a little girl whose neck, forehead, and ears are covered with black dye, shows me a *chitonti,* a native skirt with a beautifully embroidered pattern in rich colors.

When I try to bargain with her, she laughs, but she is firm about the price. "This *chitonti* took a month to make," she says.

I pay her what she wants.

With stores in Pucallpa selling cloth, spinning cotton is as rare these days as the practice of tying boards to babies' foreheads to flatten them. Only in remote villages is a mildly flattened forehead still considered a sign of beauty.

We arrive at Nuevo Destino, a larger village of dusty huts. The soccer field has patches of green breaking through the earth. Clotheslines hang between the huts.

At first glance, aside from children who gather round me with hands outstretched for gifts, the village looks deserted, but couples are lying quietly in the shade of their huts.

Angel approaches a woman painting a large piece of cotton cloth. "Do you have any pots?" he asks her. "The gringa is looking for pots."

Shaking her head no, she continues painting a lightly sketched pattern with a sliver of bark dipped in a bowl of dark pigment. I sit on her raised palm floor and watch. There is a stillness about her like the stillness of trees.

The artists picture designs in their minds, but nothing is pre-measured. The resulting patterns, however, are perfectly proportioned and symmetrical. Everything fits. By some miracle all the lines come out evenly spaced like the pattern being painted here.

Until 200 years ago, designs covered every surface in the villages, from the houses and boats to kitchen utensils. Even their faces, hands, and legs were painted with designs. The patterns were never repeated. The elements were endlessly recombined as they still are today, but now the designs are limited to pottery and cloth.

The Shipibo believe the most perfect designs exist in the heavens. In Shipibo myth, Ronin, the Great World boa, the giver of life, permeates the universe, encircling it with her spiral body. The shaman takes the hallucinogen, *ayahuasca,* to see the designs in the heavens. In songs, he calls the invisible patterns from the spirit world to descend on the village to heal the sick. The women make these healing designs visible.

The designs are mainly decorative now, but they are thought to derive from the human figure, even though the patterns resemble snake skin. Most of the original meanings of the elements are said to be lost.

As I watch the woman paint, I think of those moments when I am making a collage and every element falls into place as if by magic. At those times, I am in harmony with the world. As artists, these women are not so foreign to me.

20

We are moving sluggishly through a canal, carpeted with hyacinth so thick I feel as though I could walk across the water. Birds cry out in the silence as Angel slashes through the tangled weeds. A squirrel monkey watches from the limb of a tree. We've been traveling downstream for several hours. Angel promised me a real hike today. Yesterday we found nothing but *chacras,* cut and burned fields, near the villages.

Up ahead, Angel points out a clearing. "We will hike there," he says.

On top of the bank stands a wood and thatch shack behind a grove of coconut palms laden with fruit. When Angel calls out, an elderly man in a straw hat appears in the doorway. Chickens scurry across the clearing, and more chickens squawk in a pen beneath the shack.

"He knows this area," Angel says to me.

"Yes, I know the area," the old man says in Spanish, "but there's not much jungle left around here. If you want jungle, you have to go three, four, maybe five days downstream. Here, the loggers have cut down many trees, and there's a lot of farming now, but I can take you on some old loggers' trails if you like."

Angel smiles at me sheepishly.

"Let's go," I say, but I feel disappointed.

I follow them down an overgrown trail into a forest with large gaps between the trees.

"During the rainy season loggers float the timber down the canals," the old man says.

Once loggers open trails to transport trees, settlers follow who cut down more timber to plant their crops. After a few years of harvests, the nutrients are used up because the settlers deplete the soil. Often, they don't have enough land to rotate crops which are geared to the market in Lima. Day-to-day survival takes precedence over what's good for the land. The settlers don't allow land to lie fallow for more than two or three years, which isn't time enough for regeneration. When the fallow period is too short, grasses and shrubs grow instead of the original forest. When the soil is depleted, the settlers move on to new areas which they cut, burn, and plant, repeating the cycle after leaving wastelands behind them.

The Bragantina zone in Brazil, one of the oldest settlement areas in the Amazon, is now considered a semi-desert: the result of uncontrolled slash-and-burn farming and the short fallow method.

Scientists, who once considered native farming primitive, now see the value of the slash-and-burn technique: the Indians allow a long fallow period between harvests.

If the forests were managed properly, they could eventually yield a higher income than cutting them down. Native trees could be harvested so they would grow back quickly. Other products could be extracted or grown on plantations without disturbing the forests; among them, rubber, quinine, coffee, houseplants, and fruit in the thousands. No one knows how many more foods, drugs, fibers, and materials will be discovered, especially in the forest canopy which is still unexplored.

This forest is a sad sight. Between the thin veil of trees, there is a dense undergrowth of grasses, weeds, and shrubs. Trees lie haphazardly on the ground. There are stumps everywhere. The valuable trees are gone. It seems strange to see sunlight in an Amazon forest.

Surprisingly, there are still some birds and animals. In the branch of a tree, Angel points out a kinkajou, or honeybear, a member of the racoon family with a prehensile tail.

Further on, we hear the harsh screeching of a hoatzin, perhaps the strangest bird in the Amazon. Born with claws at the tips of its wings, the pheasant-like hoatzin may be the missing link in the evolution from reptiles to birds.

"There is something I want to show you," the old man says. He cuts across the trail, beckoning me to follow. I stumble through the thickets after him. This is as bad as walking through a *chacra.*

We come to a large tree lying on the ground. The old man helps me up onto the trunk which must be a hundred feet long. When we reach a cross section, the old man climbs down on a bough.

"This tree was cut down just for the honey," he says. "All the hives were taken but this one."

He points to a cavity in the trunk. I watch in horror as he sticks his head inside.

"They don't sting," he says, as a score of melipona bees — the smallest honey bees I've ever seen — circle his head.

"Come and look," he says.

The walls of the dark cavity are lined with honeycombs. In the combs, the golden red substance smells sickly sweet. The loud buzz of worker bees echoes in the chamber.

Melipona bees feed on tree sap and bird dung more often than flowers. The great naturalist Henry Walter Bates said they don't sting, but they "furiously bite" anyone who disturbs their hive.

We continue through the undergrowth until we reach a trail that cuts between a large *chacra*. A blue-crowned motmot flies across the black spires of burnt trees.

Ascending hilly ground, we come upon a logger's shack. I see my first beer cans lying in Amazon forest. The labels advertise the Pucallpa brewery.

Flying over the Amazon from Lima, I saw miles and miles of unspoilt jungle. I thought perhaps scientists were exaggerating. The destruction didn't seem real until now.

Late in the day as we dock at Puerto Callao and I say goodbye to Angel, I notice the greens of the trees have a coppery cast.

Along the dirt road by the lake at the edge of town, there is a tiny zoo set back behind the trees. Perhaps the time of day makes it seem so magical. This small secret place fills me with the wonder I've been missing here until now.

In a little wire mesh cage, a toucan surprises me with its frog-like croak. In the dimming light, I bypass the other animals to get a good look at the sloth. One claw with three hook-like talons clutches the cage, while its head, shaped like a flying saucer, moves slowly from side to side like a bottle cap unscrewing. One leg moves slowly downward like a mechanical toy with a dying battery. The sloth doesn't notice when its baby dies from a fall. Even a gun shot will elicit no response. With green-tinged algae growing on its back to disguise it from enemies, the sloth survives without fear or curiosity, perfectly adapted to its life in the forest.

I look at the sloth's expressionless face and dull eyes until darkness erases its features. How could such a strange animal live on this earth?

But my sense of wonder doesn't last long. In Puerto Callao I still feel like a train that can't find the right track.

On impulse, I visit Antonio at the hotel after dinner. He pulls up a chair for me in front of the TV.

"You are enjoying Yarinacocha?" he asks, in his gravelly voice, over the din of the television in the darkened room.

On the TV an affluent-looking young couple advertise furniture. Shouting to make myself heard, I reply, "Not much." Maybe this was a bad idea. "If there's a program you want to watch, I'll come back another time."

"No, no," he says. "Make yourself comfortable."

"Could you turn that down?" I ask, pointing to the TV. I wonder why these people love noise.

Lowering the TV, he says, "You have to relax to enjoy Yarina. You aren't relaxed. People who live in cities don't know how to relax. They always need something to do. Here, there is nothing to do but enjoy the peace and quiet. If you want excitement, go some place else. There's no excitement here.

"My ex-wife lives in Lima. So does my married daughter and my son, who goes to college. But I will never leave the jungle." He shakes his mop of white hair. "I like to see happy smiling faces."

"I haven't seen many happy smiling faces," I say to him.

"Did you ever look at the faces of Indians from the Andes?" he says. "They are always sad. Even their music is sad. You will never see faces like that in the jungle. You will never hear such sad music."

"Here, the Indians are angry, not sad," I say to him, but he ignores my comment and gets up in his bedroom slippers to pour himself a drink.

"Do you want one?" he asks.

"No thanks."

"Make an old man happy. Have a drink with me," he says, smiling. "Maybe we can make beautiful music together."

"I don't think so," I say, laughing.

"Even an old man can dream," he says, with a shrug.

"I think I'll be going now."

"You're not leaving because of anything I said? You know I'm harmless, don't you?"

"Yes, I know," I say, smiling.

Before I leave, I let him give me a fatherly hug.

Restless, I walk to the waterfront. Antonio is right. I don't know how to relax. I don't know what to do here. The thought of taking a long river trip is as unappealing now as it was before. I feel ambivalent about visiting more Shipibo villages. I feel as though my presence chips away at their world. The Shipibo aren't interested in me. They see only my gifts and my money. I'm an intruder like the missionaries who lured the Indians with presents and created a need in them for the goods of civilization, those goods that promoted theft and rivalry.

Before missionaries came, they had everything they needed. Amazonian Indians prospered for thousands of years without machetes, metal pots, and the other gifts they grew to crave. They lived without the material goals of our culture. They lived in harmony with nature.

I don't see any point in being here. Why stay longer? There's a flight to Lima tomorrow afternoon. While I muse I notice two hazy figures walking up the bank.

"Lucy! What are you doing here?" I call out.

"Ooh, I'm so sick!" the English girl says, clinging to her guide, Felipe.

"What happened?" I ask, putting my arm around her shoulder as she sways. Her skin feels as though she's on fire.

"It was the sun," she says weakly, as we slowly walk toward Antonio's hotel. "Felipe told me not to sit in the sun without a hat, but there was a breeze on the water. The sun didn't bother me." She closes her eyes for a moment. "I felt fine until last night when we camped on the beach. Since then the world is spinning."

"She has a bad case of river sickness," Felipe says, his face grave.

"Felipe's been terrific," Lucy says, with effort. "We made it back in record time."

Inside Antonio's room, she collapses in a chair. I feel concerned about Lucy. Despite the two dark stumps which are his teeth, Felipe's smile reassures me. At least Lucy found a sympathetic guide.

In the dim light, Lucy's eyes are glazed and her fair skin looks bright pink. Antonio, his face grim, studies her closely.

"Don't worry. I'll make you well," he says, in his low, hoarse voice.

His eyes close and he slowly passes his hand back and forth over Lucy's head. When his hand hovers directly above her, one of his fingers vibrates with a life of its own. Antonio opens his eyes after several minutes and watches his quivering finger as though the appendage belongs to someone else. Felipe and I look on in silence. Lucy's eyes are closed. A few minutes later Antonio removes his hand.

"How do you feel?" he asks Lucy.

Opening her eyes, she looks as though she's just awakened from a deep sleep. For a long moment she looks at Antonio in silence. "I feel fine," she says, barely believing her words. "What did you do?" she asks him. The sparkle is back in her eyes though she still seems weak.

"Get some sleep," Antonio says. "You'll be fine in the morning."

Felipe and I escort her to a bungalow.

"That man is amazing!" Lucy says to us at the door.

Standing in the darkness with Felipe, I stare at Lucy in wonder, though Felipe doesn't seem surprised. Perhaps Felipe is used to miracles. But I have never seen a *curandero* in action before.

21

I walk to the zoo this morning, looking for a reason to stay. I'm looking for a moment of magic, but I know the odds of finding it are slim. Instead of magic I find a barefoot boy sweeping the marmoset cage. While the marmosets scream, the boy cuts up a banana and scoops out the seeds from a papaya for their breakfast. Nearby, three coatis — members of the racoon family — madly chase each other back and forth in their trembling cage.

I return to the hotel and knock on Lucy's door.

"How do you feel?" I ask her.

"I'm fine," Lucy says, zipping up her knapsack, "but I've had enough of this place. There's a monstrous black spider somewhere in this room. I hope it hasn't crawled inside my backpack. I don't want to take it with me to Lima."

"I may go back to Lima, too," I say to her, "but I hate to end my trip feeling disappointed, and today's my birthday. I want to buy myself a present. Maybe I can persuade the couple at the Shipibo co-op to sell me a pot on exhibition. Want to come?"

"Sure," Lucy replies. "Maybe I can find something for my mum."

At the market, I tell the Shipibo couple I will buy a painted cloth — of better quality than the pots for sale — if they will sell me two bowls from the exhibition. I get my way.

I am so engrossed in choosing my Shipibo bowls I have almost forgotten the decision I still must make.

At Wilfredo's restaurant, Margrit and Vicente invite us to join them for lunch as a boy with a large moving sack tries to sell Vicente a capuchin monkey. Vicente shakes his head no, but the boy is persistent.

"I'm glad you found a friend who speaks your language," Margrit says about Lucy who has left us to say goodbye to Soledad at the lodge.

Along with the heat, humidity, and mosquitoes (fortunately, the chiggers have left me alone), speaking Spanish saps my energy, too, especially when I have to discourage people like the boy with the monkey, who thinks I can't resist the little face peering out of the sack.

"It must get lonely here alone," Margrit says, ignoring the monkey.

"I wouldn't mind being alone if I felt some connection here. But I can't seem to get my bearings in this place," I say to her, as the boy with the monkey fastens his hopes on the next table.

"So this is the end of your trip?" she asks.

"I don't see any point in staying," I tell her.

As I leave the table I notice the boy with the monkey has made a sale.

A while later, Lucy and I enter Antonio's office, ready to leave. "You're going so soon?" he asks, surprised.

When he throws his arms around me, I realize I'll miss the old man.

From the cab Puerto Callao looks better than usual.

At the airport I'm surprised to see the crowds so tame.

"What a queue!" Lucy says, as we walk to the end of the line.

"Maybe I shouldn't leave," I say to her. "It feels too easy. I don't like giving up."

"What would you do if you stayed?" Lucy asks.

"I'd take a river trip with Felipe. I'd look for the finest Shipibo pots."

I see now that I haven't been honest with myself. I've been more afraid here than I've been willing to admit. I haven't allowed myself to be open except at odd moments.

In the cab back to Puerto Callao I feel lightheaded. Something inside me has snapped into place. When I arrived here, I wanted to hang on to the wonderful feelings I had in Iquitos. I didn't want another challenge. The more I resisted everything around me, the worse everything looked. I've been reacting to circumstances, looking for something or someone outside myself to make this trip a success.

Antonio laughs when he sees me. "You couldn't stay away," he says, hugging me again.

I find Felipe on his boat in the harbor and arrange a river trip for tomorrow morning.

If I think of my visits to Shipibo villages as my way to support their art, I feel less intrusive. After all, Shipibo artists welcome the income.

After dinner the air cools. A breeze blowing over the lake gathers force. But I am no longer dependent on the weather. Tomorrow I will leave on the river, rain or shine.

I write in my journal by the port, under a swaying bulb. Moths circle the light like moons orbiting a planet while the real moon stares out between the clouds. Live music plays in one of the bars. I've never heard music like this. I walk over. A woman beckons to me. "Come," she says, smiling.

Inside, some women offer me juice laced with *aquadiente*. I sit among women and children on stools lining the walls, listening to the poignant melodies of a flutist, accompanied by two grave-faced drummers who slowly bang the old drums. Two women cross themselves before pictures of the Virgin on a makeshift altar draped with purple crepe paper. Candle flames throw shadows on the walls, decorated with pinups. The two women begin to dance. More women join them. Men gather in the doorway. Like Pied Pipers, the musicians circle the room, leading a stream of dancers. When the musicians return to their places, the men choose partners. The room spins with swirling skirts.

I am taking in the music, the dancing. I am feeling that sense of life I missed. That life was here all along, but I couldn't feel it. I didn't see that I had cut myself off.

This morning I feel excited meeting Felipe and his young pilot, Bonifacio, on the boat. For the first time since I arrived the air is cool and clear.

We dock on the lake near a cluster of shacks not far from Puerto Callao. This village called San José is Felipe's home.

A ramp on stilts connects his three shacks of unplaned planks. I find it odd to see padlocked doors since the window screens are torn and the thatched roofs are full of holes.

His young wife, Esperanza, makes me a breakfast of fried eggs with crackers while the men load the *pegue-pegue* with supplies.

She holds a baby in her arms.

"How many children do you have?" I ask her.

"Two," she replies.

"That's all?" I say, without thinking. I expected her to say eight or nine.

On the boat there is hardly room for me among the moldy mattresses, fishing nets, mosquito nets, petrol drums, cooking pots, food, and kegs of drinking water, but Felipe adjusts a mattress so I sit like a queen on a moldy throne.

Shortly after we enter the canals that lead to the Ucayali River, the heavy boat gets stuck. I watch Felipe rock the boat loose. He was probably handsome when he was young, but now his face is lined, and his loose skin looks like dried-out leather.

When we reach the open water, Felipe joins me at the prow.

"Lucy felt well when she left?" he asks.

"Yes," I reply.

"She never complained once when she was sick," Felipe says. "She's a strong girl. She's had a hard life."

"What do you mean?" I ask him.

"Her father killed himself," Felipe says.

"She told you that?" I ask, surprised.

"Yes," he says. "We became very close."

A few hours on the Ucayali River is enough to numb the liveliest mind. My excitement has vanished with the cool air which is only a memory by midday. On the far banks, the trees, the occasional huts, the sandbars, the islands in the wide, serpentine river seem to repeat themselves like a film loop. Even the birds seem to repeat their paths in the sky. There is an advantage, however, to my present frame of mind: I'm not wishing I were somewhere else. I'm not wishing for anything. The numbness makes it easy to accept the way things are.

We stop along the river for lunch at a small mestizo settlement where a friend of Felipe's owns a restaurant. The thatched-roof shack with half-walls of bamboo has a table with a bench in the center. A kerosene stove stands in a corner.

Felipe's friend, a man past fifty with a huge potbelly and a hooked nose reaching to his mouth, asks me, "Is there a restaurant in the United States that looks like this?"

"I haven't seen one," I admit, as his wife serves us chicken and rice.

Two grown sons enter the hut and sit on stools by the wall, watching us.

"I have seven more children," he says, proudly. "How many do you have?"

When I tell him I have neither children nor a husband, he looks at me with pity in his eyes.

A while later on the river, when Felipe calls out "Alligators!" I think of Henry Walter Bates, who in the nineteenth century compared the alligators in Brazil's Solimões River during the dry season to swarming tadpoles in an English ditch in summer.

What Felipe is referring to, however, are three healthy-looking specimens sunbathing on a slab of mud, with jaws large enough to swallow my lower leg in one gulp.

In drier parts of the Amazon, alligators sleep through the dry season, but here they are active all year. After the rubber boom, when the Ucayali was more populated than the Amazon, and former rubber tappers settled here to plant cotton or catch *paiche* and turtles, most of the animals were frightened away. But the large alligators remained.

There may be more to see than I thought. Just above the waterline, I see bullet-like holes on the bank made by *cuiu-cuiu*, a catfish that sucks its prey out of mud.

As the boat turns onto the smaller Calleria River, a Ucayali tributary, the cry of a bird, a bellbird perhaps, sounds like a hammer hitting iron.

At Patria Nueva, a Shipibo village hidden behind forest, the huts look decrepit. One hut, struck by a storm, has collapsed. Dogs and chickens wander about. Smoke rises from cooking fires. Large water jars painted with designs look odd beside plastic pails from Pucallpa.

As usual, the children badger me for gifts; but, unfortunately, many of the pens I give to them have dried out. I have barely enough to go round. The father of a small boy asks for a black pen instead of the blue one I gave to his son. The father is satisfied when I find one that works, but the children plead for more. They follow me through the village, whining, while their parents look on in silence.

Their wailing reminds me of the ragged children in Marrakesh years ago, who followed my husband and me through the native quarter, pleading for money. In exasperation, my husband emptied his pockets of change. The children dove for the coins like wild beasts.

I'm too distracted by these children to look for pots, so we return to the boat.

Further along the river, Felipe offers a lift to a Shipibo woman paddling a tiny canoe with five children. The canoe is the only boat we've seen for hours.

I make room for the children on my mattress, while Felipe ties their dugout to our boat.

The mosquitoes are fierce. I've been dousing myself with repellent. I feel sorry for these children, their arms and legs covered with bites, some oozing pus, but I also feel repelled watching the oldest girl pick lice from her little brother's hair. Felipe laughs at me when I shake out the mattress, after dropping them off on the bank.

Sitting down beside me, Felipe says, bitterly, "Nobody cares about people in the jungle. Candidates don't even come here before elections.

"Lima takes from the jungle, but gives nothing back. We make Lima rich with lumber and oil, but we see none of that money. We need schools, hospitals, roads. But officials fill their pockets with our taxes.

"Peru has always depended on stronger countries. First Spain, then England, now we sell our products cheap to the United States. Peru will never learn to stand on its own."

He pauses for a moment. "This doesn't matter to you," he says, smiling, but there is an unpleasant edge in his voice. "You live in a rich country. You come here on vacation. You forget about the jungle when you go home."

"I care what happens here," I say to him, but he is not convinced.

22

On the sandbar where we are camped, the mosquitoes are vicious after dark. I crawl under my mosquito net and lie on my thin damp mattress waiting for dinner. I've used up all my repellent except for a Peruvian brand.

I discover during dinner the Peruvian brand doesn't work. Covered with bites after a hasty meal of fish and burnt rice, I retreat to my net and find my Peruvian flashlight batteries don't work either, though I bought them from a store in Iquitos that sold nothing but flashlights.

Lying in darkness with nothing to do but slap my bites — scratching leads to infections — I wallow in self-pity, which makes me feel worse.

Once again, I'm allowing circumstances beyond my control to throw me off balance. Instead of feeling sorry for myself, I should be happy I haven't seen any vampire bats. I decide to accept the fact that there is nothing I can do about the mosquitoes or the darkness. Now I feel better. Even my bites feel better. I doze off.

This morning, a few feet from my mosquito net, Felipe tells me to freeze. I look down and see a small coiled snake. Felipe beats the brownish snake over the head with a stick. "His venom would have killed you," he says.

The snake, however, bothers me less than the mosquitoes, which are so fierce I don't dare bathe. After a quick breakfast of fish I am glad to pack up and head out on the river.

There are no surprises on the river this morning, but Felipe surprises me by taking a rifle from the clutter of supplies, along with a machete and two fishing poles, as Bonifacio pulls up to the bank where Felipe and I will hike.

"Why are you taking a rifle?" I ask him.

"For the snakes and ocelots," he says.

I'm glad we're far enough away from Puerto Callao to hike in jungle, though Felipe has to drag me up the almost vertical slope. It's just as well I haven't bathed. I feel as though I'm sinking in quicksand.

On the trail we disturb a large iguana which bounds to the ground with a great rustling sound.

Felipe slashes the bark of a tree and shows me a thick, white sap, a deadly poison if ingested. If it touches the skin, he says, it causes incurable sores.

Further along the trail, he shows me how to drink the cool, fresh water that spouts from a vine as thick as my arm. The vine draws water from the ground and purifies it. Felipe says, "People die of thirst in the jungle because they don't know about this vine."

On and on we walk until we come to a lake, covered with

hyacinth. Down below a dugout lies by the shore.

"We will fish there," Felipe says, pointing to the open water at the far end of the lake.

But the thick, tangled weeds resist the paddles. A quarter of an hour later, our efforts have moved us only a few feet from shore. "It would take two weeks to reach that open water," I say, laughing, but Felipe doesn't look amused.

Before we continue down the trail, he goes off to relieve himself.

I only need to be alone for twenty minutes here to feel small, insignificant, vulnerable. I think of my busy life at home, always driven to accomplish, always trying to be special. The Amazon may be the mother of life, but she doesn't play favorites. I'm not special here. No amount of striving will win her affirmation. In this world one form of life is no more important than another. Here, I am a human being among leaves, ants, vines.

I hear a branch break. I hear rustling leaves and the buzzing of insects. As the minutes pass, I sense something sinister in the heavy stillness. How quickly fear severs my connection to the jungle. I look at my watch. Felipe's been gone more than thirty-minutes.

"Felipe!" I call out. But all I hear is the rustling of dead leaves. What would I do if he didn't come back? We're more than two hours away from the river.

At last I hear steps, his steps, I hope!

"I was worried," I say to him, but he just laughs.

Later, on the river, we stop to cook a midday meal on a sandbar. The sand is as smooth as a baby's skin except where water has receded at the edge, leaving the imprint of little rippling waves.

Felipe and I bathe in the shallow but swiftly moving water.

"Is there a river in New York?" Felipe asks.

"Yes," I reply.

"Is there high and low water like the Amazon?" he asks.

"No, there are high and low tides, but the river doesn't flood like the Amazon," I say.

Felipe looks surprised.

While the men cook a distance away, I write in my journal on the boat, barely aware of tiny flies gathering round me until I am engulfed by a thick, black cloud. Before I fully realize what is happening, hundreds of tiny punctures appear on my arms, my legs, my ankles. The bites itch like mad.

When a horde of mosquitoes accompany the men carrying pots of steaming food, I reach my limit. "For God's sake, let's eat somewhere else!" I say, angrily. I see the sandbar with different eyes. It no longer looks so clean and pure. Here, nothing is the way it seems.

On the Pachitea river, another Ucayali tributary, a low rumbling like thunder draws my eyes to the bank in time to see a large chunk of earth, complete with trees, collapsing into the river, sending clouds of spray high in the air. Large waves rock the boat. For a moment I am reminded of the amusement parks where my father took me when I was a child. I feel the same excitement I felt on the Tilt-A-Whirl and the roller coaster.

But by the time we arrive at the dusty village of Pachitea, I feel my usual numbness. The settlement stands on top of the steepest bank. I don't envy the Shipibo climbing up and down several times a day to bathe or fish or wash clothes.

Felipe says they don't sell pottery here, though I see some large *chomos*, ceramic storage jars about three feet high used for manioc beer, which is drunk in great quantities at fiestas. To make the brew, the women chew the yucca root and mix it with their saliva, then spit it out into a large wooden trough. The mass ferments in the sun for two or three days before the liquid is strained into the large ceramic jars.

The only Shipibo who shows any interest in my visit is a woman suffering from menstrual cramps who asks me for pills.

We camp on another sandbar toward sundown, but the mosquitoes are as vicious here as the ones the night before.

To avoid the insects, we leave before dawn. Bonifacio, who slept on the boat, was bitten by a vampire bat during the night. His big toe is all bloody. The bat managed to bite through his sneaker.

I feel almost faint from the heat as I follow Felipe down the path to the village of Saposoa. Beside the path, a dead alligator rots by the shore. Even its tough, scaly hide is no protection from the insects. Its neck gouged, its eye sockets empty, its small legs dangle in water while flies and butterflies feast.

The village looks deserted. We pass huts with transister radios on otherwise empty floors. At the edge of the village, four barefoot children watch us approach from the shade of an unusually cluttered hut. Among their possessions, I see a stereo record player hooked up to a car battery. On a roof beam, stacks of 45 RPM records hang from hooks.

"Where is everyone?" Felipe asks the oldest girl.

"They've gone to the river to harvest rice," she replies.

"There's another stream behind this village," Felipe tells me.

I rest in the shade while Felipe buys me a coconut, which the girl shakes from a tree.

I begin to wonder if I will ever find any Shipibo pots.

The sun follows us like a hunter tracking prey on our way to the village of Calleria. The journey to this village seems to take forever.

The large settlement, with neat rows of well-built huts and wide paths, reminds me of San Francisco, fortunately, it doesn't feel like San Francisco. I don't sense hostility, but I feel that invisible wall. When I enter each village, I feel the blinds being drawn.

But here I see artists working. Almost every woman is involved in making pottery.

The women are friendly to Felipe, who laughs and jokes with them. Their high-pitched voices have a shrill, peculiar ring. I feel ill-at-ease in their presence. But I am excited to see them at work.

The bare-breasted woman who covers herself as we approach, kneads clay in a large, wooden trough while sitting cross-legged on the ground. Looking at her and another woman in her hut building a pot with snake-like clay coils — the oldest pottery technique known — makes me feel as though I am witnessing prehistory.

The shapes of Shipibo pots follow traditional forms, but each woman has a slightly different touch, resulting in minor variations. But the true skill and imagination of the women is tested in the painting of designs that continues to be a living and growing tradition.

In Shipibo designs, the spaces are filled. Between heavy lines are fine lines. Not all designs are complex, but in the most intricate ones, I see the chaos of the jungle arranged in orderly patterns.

The women use standard motifs which must follow certain rules. Their creativity arises from and within these limitations that force them to find new variations. Often, women will travel to a distant village to copy designs from a respected artist, but the copies are always different from the original, and are used for inspiration.

Each woman creates her own repertoire of unique designs, collected since childhood, when her mother trained her to be an artist. A general sense of style is handed down from mother to daughter.

Shipibo modesty keeps women from praising their own work. They also refrain from praising each other's work openly because that would mean the critic knows more than the artist. But the Shipibo have definite likes and dislikes. A bad design is one that is obvious, whereas an imaginative design transcends or obscures the basic plan whether delicate and detailed or simplified and bold. They look also for care and control in the painting.

Watching a woman paint evenly spaced lines on the curved surface of a bowl with a brush made from her hair, I understand why the Shipibo keep the best pots for themselves or give them away as gifts. They deserve a better fate than being sold casually as souvenirs in airports.

I've seen few finished pieces. I thought that even here I might not find the pots I want, so I am excited to see a hut with many bowls and potbellied jars. When I take a closer look, I see I've hit the jackpot! I've found a very gifted artist. These pots have paper-thin walls. They feel like egg shells in my hands. They have black and brown and brick red designs, with crosses and diamonds and triangles and curvilinear shapes on cream-colored backgrounds.

I've seen perfection over and over in the Amazon. I've seen it in small things. But here, for the first time, I find the perfection I found in nature in these objects made by human hands. I find perfection in a stone, a window, a quiet street, a teapot, a line of poetry, the veins in a leaf. At home I have books and sea shells, stones and fossils and other objects that partake of this perfection, so I can look up from my busyness and get a glimpse of what is real to me in the world.

I wish I could buy all these jars and bowls, but I limit myself to choosing four.

The artist, a middle-aged woman with a strong face and mocking eyes, seems mildly amused by my enthusiasm. Perhaps her sense of modesty keeps her from acknowledging my praise, but I am more inclined to think my opinion doesn't matter very much to her. She seems slightly annoyed when she has to interrupt her conversation with relatives to tell me the prices of the bowls I've chosen.

"Ninety *inti* each," she says.

When I try to bargain, she snaps, "The price is low enough."

I try to recall who told me the Shipibo love to bargain, as I carefully carry my treasures back to the boat.

23

Felipe is annoyed with me for staying so long in Calleria. He didn't want to be on the river after dark. The light fades shortly after we leave the village on our way to Tacshitea, a settlement at the mouth of the Calleria River where we will spend the night.

Bonifacio seems to guide the boat by instinct. He says the water is very shallow in spots. He proves his point when the boat gets stuck on a sandbank.

In the moonlight, the water looks deep purple and sparkles with amethyst highlights. Fireflies glimmer in the air. Dolphins leap past us in the deeper water in gleaming violet arcs.

The men grunt and heave, pitting themselves against the boat which refuses to budge for nearly an hour.

As I follow the men across the wide moonlit beach at Tacshitea to the huts above the high bank, I can feel that Felipe is still annoyed with me. But these nights on the river have forced me to depend more on myself and less on circumstance. It would be nice if Felipe liked me as much as he liked Lucy, but I can live with his annoyance. It won't spoil my night.

Felipe greets a Shipibo woman who invites us inside her hut. In the kerosene light, I see children crawling on the floor.

After speaking to the woman, Felipe says, "We can sleep in an empty hut or we can sleep on the beach again. What do you want to do?"

I recall a story Kenneth told me. On the river he usually slept in a hut with the Shipibo, but one night he was offered the honor of sleeping alone in a hut where grain was stored. As soon as he lay down in his sleeping bag, rats attacked his mosquito net. Using his gear to protect his head, he dozed off until a blast of radio music jolted him awake. Outside, three loggers full of beer, with rifles and chains of bullets slung across their chests, had rekindled a dying Shipibo fire. Half-awake and beside himself, Kenneth threatened the loggers. They laughed at him because he didn't have a gun. He was lucky, he said. A murder that far upriver would never be reported.

"Let's sleep on the beach," I say to Felipe. Even drunken loggers with rifles seem preferable to rats.

I am left alone while the men fish for dinner. I walk along the beach, watching the full moon rise over the water. I've never seen the moon so large. It stares straight at me like a luminous, all-seeing eye, casting its silvery spell over the sand and the water. I am drawn to this moon like insects to light.

Doors swing open inside me. I stand like the moon's mansion, full of windows reflecting her silvery light.

A song comes to mind, a song from summer camp many years ago that I sang in celebration. I learned in summer camp to take care of myself. When I arrived, I was the only camper who couldn't tie her shoes, make her bed, or fold her clothes. I was helpless and shy. But by the end of that summer, I felt a sense of satisfaction, a sense of freedom like the freedom I am feeling now.

I sing my song softly at first, but as I sing I feel myself expand. My song grows louder. It fills the air and embraces the moon and the sand and the river. The world has opened itself to me because I have opened myself to life. I am filled with happiness and gratitude.

> The silver moon is shining
> upon the golden meadow.
> I walk up and down the meadow
> with no one near me.
>
> How lovely is the moonlight
> between the shadows breaking.
> My heart will cease its aching
> If Thou art with me.

This is how I always dreamed the moon would be. In this moon I see that my dream is real.

The Shipibo woman cooks our dinner on the beach. While Felipe and Bonifacio laugh with her, I look out at the water in the silvery light, and up at the sky with its satiny sheen where even the stars look polished.

By the light of the kerosene lantern, I write in my journal after dinner. I try to ignore the mosquitoes, but with every line I write, I chase them from my head and hands.

One of the Shipibo woman's sons, a boy about fifteen who has wandered down to our camp, sits on the sand beside me.

"Hello," he says, smiling.

"You speak English?" I ask, surprised.

"I study English," he says. "I know many words." He recites a list of English words for me, then reverts to Spanish. "What are you writing?" he asks.

"I'm writing about my trip," I say to him.

"Can I see? I am learning to read English, too," he says.

I flip through the pages. I find a section with a little story about a hummingbird. "Can you read this?" I ask.

He reads the English words out loud as best he can, but then he laughs, and says, "I don't understand."

I try to translate the words into Spanish. He helps me look in my dictionary for words I don't know.

"Shall I try to tell you the story in Spanish?" I ask him.

"Oh, yes," he says, excitedly.

The boy, whose name is Macario, sits very close to me. He gazes into my eyes, eagerly awaiting my words. I begin.

"Some houseboys found a tiny hummingbird in the garden of the hotel in Iquitos. The houseboys thought the bird couldn't fly. They found a tiny cage for the bird, but they didn't close the door because the hummingbird didn't move. The houseboys watched the hummingbird for several minutes until they grew bored and went to do their chores. But when one of the boys returned, he saw the hummingbird flying madly around the cage, the door shut. He called his buddies together. 'Who closed the door?' he asked. All of them shook their heads. The guests weren't in their rooms, so none of the guests closed the door. As the houseboys looked at the hummingbird and wondered, a great gust of wind blew into the garden. 'The wind closed the door!' the boys cried. When one of them opened the cage, they all watched as the hummingbird flew away, but still they wondered why the bird didn't move when they found it."

Macario, who looks spellbound, comes to life at the end of my tale. He laughs and claps his hands.

"How many nights will you stay here?" he asks.

"Two," I reply.

"I wish you would stay longer," he says.

"Maybe I will. Where do you study English?" I ask him.

"I go to secondary school," he says, proudly.

"Is there one in Tacshitea?" I ask.

"Oh, no. I must paddle very far to get there. Tell me more stories," he says, smiling.

I flip through my journal for inspiration. "One very hot day," I begin, "an American man decided that he needed a swim to cool off. From a high point on the bank, he dove into the river, but the current was much stronger than he expected, and carried him so fast he was soon out of the sight of his friends back at camp. A large log drifted downstream beside him. The man thought he was going crazy when he heard a voice say, 'Just hang on to me. I will take you back.' The man listened to the log and grabbed hold. Suddenly the log changed direction and raced against the current, taking him back to his camp. When the log stopped by the muddy bank, the man thanked the log and ran up the steep slope to tell his friends. But his friends were angry because he had made them so worried. 'You must be crazy to try to swim in that river!' they told him. The man said nothing about the log which saved his life. He began to wonder if the log was only a dream. He began to wonder if he really was crazy."

Macario laughs and claps his hands again.

"What will you do when you finish school?" I ask him.

"I will marry and become the teacher in my village."

"Do you have a girlfriend?"

"Yes, she is fifteen. I am sixteen. Next year we will marry."

"How many children are there in your family?"

"I have seven sisters and two brothers," Macario says. "I am the oldest. How old are you?"

"I'm probably older than your mother."

"Really?"

"How old is your mother?" I ask.

"Thirty-eight."

"I'm forty-one," I say to him.

Macario laughs. "I want to read more in your book," he says.

I look for something in my journal that I think will interest him. I find the part where Luis spots a baby ocelot at night. As Macario reads I translate the words into Spanish. Laughing together in the flickering light of the lantern, we read more pages. Even the mosquitoes don't bother me. When Macario smiles and looks into my eyes with such openness, I wonder if I could feel closer to a son than I feel to this boy I just met on the beach. The closeness we share seems as magical as the moon.

While we huddle by the light I turn around and find the beach deserted. His mother has gone. Felipe has retired under the mosquito net, and Bonifacio is asleep on the boat. When I look at my watch, I'm amazed to see it's almost 2 AM Macario and I have been sitting here for hours!

"I've been having such a good time I had no idea it was this late," I say to him.

"I've had a very good time," Macario says, smiling. He places his hand on my shoulder as we say goodnight. As he heads for his hut, I watch his dim form disappear in the darkness while the silvery moon, smaller now, watches us from a different angle in the sky.

24

After spending two more nights on the river, I thought I would sleep for a week, but I am wide-awake in my room in Puerto Callao at 3 AM. In the days following our meeting, I saw Macario for only a few minutes. His hut wasn't far from our camp, but each day mosquitoes and biting flies forced me under my mosquito net at sundown. Each day we rose before dawn and left quickly. The days were long. On the river it was too hot to think. I was tired. I was dirty. I felt as though I had seen everything before. I reached my limit. I was ready to go home.

When I arrived in the jungle, I thought about the Amazon in relation to myself and my needs. I had a dream to make real.

In between these moments of seeing my dream in the world, I

began to see the jungle with different eyes. My revulsion in Puerto Callao made me aware of an Amazon I didn't want to see. This Amazon had nothing to do with my dream.

I had come to the Amazon to experience life in its raw state. In Puerto Callao life is raw, but this rawness is not what nature intended. This rawness results from thoughtless tampering with the ecology. This is not a place that inspires fantasies of running wild in virgin jungle. Puerto Callao, with its oil spills and garbage, looks a bit too much like the vacant lots of my childhood.

The first time I was here I knew too little about the Amazon to know what I was seeing. I was reacting to my dream. This time I knew too much to overlook the damage being done. What I saw made my dream unimportant. But still it was my dream. I almost used the sorry state of Puerto Callao as my excuse for not living it. Of course, my dream isn't important the way that saving the Amazon is important, but it was my reason for being here, and now I feel the satisfaction that comes from seeing it through before the forests are destroyed.

In the five hundred years since the European discovery, men couldn't control the Amazon or its people, but technology has changed all that.

As the world becomes homeogeneous, the sights and sounds and smells and tastes in the world diminish. This leveling leads to the dulling of life, the diminishment of wonder. Looking into the faces of the Shipibo gave me a glimpse into a different way of being in the world. That glimpse into their lives aroused my wonder.

Some people can only live in a jungle that isn't a jungle anymore. The only people able to live in harmony in this one are the Indians, who leave little or no trace of themselves in the forests. The Indians never had the idea to conquer, to tame the Amazon. They lived here with nothing to prove.

Some Indians move further into the interior to escape, but eventually they will be found. Paradoxically, the more they understand our culture and how to get what they want, the more chance they will have to preserve their cultures. But their cultures are already changed by exposure to ours, and the traditions they preserve in the future will exist in a context far removed from the one in which they existed before contact with the outside world.

For me, the Amazon is more than a place. Even if men cut down the Amazon, it will still exist because there will still be an unconscious, there will still be mystery, and things that cannot be understood or controlled by the rational mind.

But in the meantime, Lake Yarinacocha is slowly turning into a sewer, which I smell from my bed as the fuzzy contours of my room emerge from darkness. I have barely closed my eyes all night, but when I rise, I feel refreshed.

I walk down the hot, dusty streets. What I see might have appeared ordinary at another time, but nothing looks ordinary now. Everything I see is invested with life, even things I find ugly: a flower-printed cloth covering a soft drink stand; aluminum pots stacked like totems outside the market. The mundane has become miraculous.

Despite the heat, the insects, the dust, the decay, I've found life that hasn't been measured, manicured, corsetted, deodorized, sanitized. Here, life hasn't been ordered in advance. Life is loose and changing form.

This is a world that may change in the blink of an eye into something else. This world is still a great magician's trick, filled with sleights of hand.

I hail a taxi to Pucallpa and reserve a seat on the afternoon flight.

Walking from the airline office, I see Soledad, George's secretary. Even off-guard she smiles.

"I thought you left," she says, surprised.

"I went on a river trip," I say to her. I am smiling, too.

"You had a good time," she says.

I laugh. "Parts of it were wonderful."

"You look very different than you did when you arrived," she says. "Your face is transparent. I can see everything you feel."

Soledad sounds more like an ancient seer than an eighteen-year-old girl. "Everything?" I say, jokingly.

"Everything," she repeats, smiling with a certainty that is almost frightening.

I ignore the slight unease she arouses in me. "I'm leaving today," I announce.

She nods with a knowing smile. "I will remember you. Will you write to me sometime? I get lonely. Everybody always leaves."

At the hotel in Puerto Callao, Antonio is curing his houseboy of some ailment. His finger quivers above the boy's head. After a few minutes, he mumbles something to the boy and sends him on his way.

"So what are you doing now?" Antonio says.

"I'm leaving," I reply.

"Again?" he laughs.

"This time I'm really leaving," I say.

"That's too bad. A nice looking gringo checked in last night. Maybe you should stay," he says, smiling.

"He arrived too late," I say, with a shrug.

The maid who watches me take Antonio's picture bursts out laughing, then covers her mouth to hide her giggles.

From the taxi I wave to Antonio with tears in my eyes.

At the crowded airport, I see the back of a man with curly hair who looks strangely familiar. When he turns slightly, I recognize his face.

"Santiago!" I gasp, running toward him.

"I don't believe it!" he cries out, throwing his arms around me. "What are you doing here?"

I feel as though I've come full circle, back to the starting point when I landed here for the first time with my guide, Santiago. What a coincidence to meet him now. He lives alone in the Andes and only leads groups to the jungle twice a year.

"You've been traveling by yourself?" he asks, his blue eyes wide with astonishment.

"Yes," I say, laughing.

"I can't wait to hear all about your trip," he says. "How long are you staying in Lima?"

"Four days. Did you stay at the lodge?" I ask him.

"Yes," he says.

"I wonder why George didn't tell me you were coming," I say, but then I remember George's interest in Lucy the night I asked about Santiago. He probably didn't hear a word I said.

Our flight is announced on the loudspeaker.

"Listen," he says, sounding almost American, "I have to rejoin my group, but my tour is over in the morning, and I'll be in Lima for a few days. Lets get together tomorrow."

As Santiago rushes through the crowd, someone calls my name. I turn and see Soledad, standing with George, waiting for the passengers from Lima to disembark.

"George has a group coming in on this flight," Soledad says, picking up one of my duffels which she carries for me over to the boarding gate. "One day I would like to take a plane all the way to New York. I have many friends there."

"I hope you will," I reply.

While Soledad dreams of going to New York, I am excited about seeing Santiago. This dream that began years ago in the vacant lots that were my jungles doesn't end in the Amazon. This dream is life.

CITY LIGHTS PUBLICATIONS

Ferlinghetti, Lawrence. PICTURES OF THE GONE WORLD
Ferlinghetti, Lawrence. SEVEN DAYS IN NICARAGUA LIBRE
Finley, Karen. SHOCK TREATMENT
Ford, Charles Henri. OUT OF THE LABYRINTH: Selected Poems
Franzen, Cola, transl. POEMS OF ARAB ANDALUSIA
García Lorca, Federico. BARBAROUS NIGHTS: Legends & Plays
García Lorca, Federico. ODE TO WALT WHITMAN & OTHER POEMS
García Lorca, Federico. POEM OF THE DEEP SONG
Ginsberg, Allen. HOWL & OTHER POEMS
Ginsberg, Allen. KADDISH & OTHER POEMS
Ginsberg, Allen. REALITY SANDWICHES
Ginsberg, Allen. PLANET NEWS
Ginsberg, Allen. THE FALL OF AMERICA
Ginsberg, Allen. MIND BREATHS
Ginsberg, Allen. PLUTONIAN ODE
Goethe, J. W. von. TALES FOR TRANSFORMATION
Hayton-Keeva, Sally, ed. VALIANT WOMEN IN WAR AND EXILE
Herron, Don. THE DASHIELL HAMMETT TOUR: A Guidebook
Herron, Don. THE LITERARY WORLD OF SAN FRANCISCO
Higman, Perry, tr. LOVE POEMS FROM SPAIN AND
        SPANISH AMERICA
Jaffe, Harold. EROS: ANTI-EROS
Jenkins, Edith. AGAINST A FIELD SINISTER
Kerouac, Jack. BOOK OF DREAMS
Kerouac, Jack. POMES ALL SIZES
Kerouac, Jack. SCATTERED POEMS
Lacarrière, Jacques. THE GNOSTICS
La Duke, Betty. COMPANERAS
La Loca. ADVENTURES ON THE ISLE OF ADOLESCENCE
Lamantia, Philip. MEADOWLARK WEST
Lamantia, Philip. BECOMING VISIBLE
Laughlin, James. SELECTED POEMS: 1935-1985
Le Brun, Annie. SADE: On the Brink of the Abyss
Lowry, Malcolm. SELECTED POEMS
Marcelin, Philippe-Thoby. THE BEAST OF THE
        HAITIAN HILLS
Masereel, Frans. PASSIONATE JOURNEY
Mayakovsky, Vladimir. LISTEN! EARLY POEMS
Mrabet, Mohammed. THE BOY WHO SET THE FIRE
Mrabet, Mohammed. THE LEMON
Mrabet, Mohammed. LOVE WITH A FEW HAIRS
Mrabet, Mohammed. M'HASHISH

Murguía, A. & B. Paschke, eds. VOLCAN: Poems from Central America
Murillo, Rosario. ANGEL IN THE DELUGE
Paschke, B. & D. Volpendesta, eds. CLAMOR OF INNOCENCE
Pasolini, Pier Paolo. ROMAN POEMS
Pessoa, Fernando. ALWAYS ASTONISHED
Peters, Nancy J., ed. WAR AFTER WAR (City Lights Review #5)
Poe, Edgar Allan. THE UNKNOWN POE
Porta, Antonio. KISSES FROM ANOTHER DREAM
Prévert, Jacques. PAROLES
Purdy, James. THE CANDLES OF YOUR EYES
Purdy, James. IN A SHALLOW GRAVE
Purdy, James. GARMENTS THE LIVING WEAR
Rachlin, Nahid. VEILS: SHORT STORIES
Rey Rosa, Rodrigo. THE BEGGAR'S KNIFE
Rey Rosa, Rodrigo. DUST ON HER TONGUE
Rigaud, Milo. SECRETS OF VOODOO
Saadawi El, Nawal. MEMOIRS OF A WOMAN DOCTOR
Sánchez, Alberto Ruy. MOGADOR
Sawyer-Lauçanno, Christopher, tr. THE DESTRUCTION OF
    THE JAGUAR
Sclauzero, Mariarosa. MARLENE
Serge, Victor. RESISTANCE
Shepard, Sam. MOTEL CHRONICLES
Shepard, Sam. FOOL FOR LOVE & THE SAD LAMENT OF
    PECOS BILL
Smith, Michael. IT A COME
Snyder, Gary. THE OLD WAYS
Solnit, Rebecca. SECRET EXHIBITION: Six California Artists
Sussler, Betsy, ed. BOMB: INTERVIEWS
Takahashi, Mutsuo. SLEEPING SINNING FALLING
Turyn, Anne, ed. TOP TOP STORIES
Tutuola, Amos. FEATHER WOMAN OF THE JUNGLE
Tutuola, Amos. SIMBI & THE SATYR OF THE DARK JUNGLE
Valaoritis, Nanos. MY AFTERLIFE GUARANTEED
Wilson, Colin. POETRY AND MYSTICISM
Zamora, Daisy. RIVERBED OF MEMORY